To: Dr. S.C.

Your gift to the body of Christ is so powerful and true, so please keep me in your prayers!

E.R. Stanton

MY PAIN, YOUR GAIN

MY PAIN, YOUR GAIN

Emile Andre Stanton

XULON PRESS

Xulon Press
2301 Lucien Way #415
Maitland, FL 32751
407.339.4217
www.xulonpress.com

Unless otherwise indicated, Scripture quotations taken from the King
James Version (KJV) – *public domain*.

Printed in the United States of America.

ISBN-13: 978-1-54566-660-9

DEDICATION

This book is dedicated to the millions of married couples (regardless of your religion), who struggle with marital issues on a daily basis and don't know how to articulate their pain. I'm just a voice crying in the wilderness, hoping that someone would dare to come from behind the walled cities and listen to a unique story that may provide a litany of fresh perspectives.

TABLE OF CONTENTS

INTRODUCTION

It is said that "experience is the best teacher," but I have found that the experience of others can be just as profitable and much less painful for any individual.

This book was birthed during a very dark period in my life, for my marriage of twenty-three years was ending, and I had lost all hope for living. I had grown very angry with God for what He had allowed to happen, simply because I couldn't fathom why this was happening to someone like me. I was very faithful to God and to my wife, yet I was somehow selected to endure such a tremendous hardship and traumatic pain.

For Christians, the rate of separation and/or divorce is traditionally swept under the rug, while we maintain the highest rate among any other group around the world. I was never interested in exploring the documented research on Christian marriages, because it was never a topic of discussion in my religious community. It wasn't until my marriage was coming to an end that I began to inquire from other Christian married couples about information on the factors of a marital breakup.

When it comes to Christian marriages, generations upon generations have remained silent and, for whatever reason, refused to share their experiences with the latter generation, making the cycle of repetition inevitable. God selected my wife and me to go through this heartbreaking experience for the sole purpose of breaking the cycle of repetition regarding Christian marriages.

Although this book captures in detail my personal experiences that led up to my marital breakdown, it is also written in hopes that it would ignite a healthy conversation to ensue about the pitfalls of Christian marriages. The fact remains that even Christian marriages are subject to real-life issues. If we don't engage in healthy discussions on the matter, we will continue to lose the marital battles. People who are engaged in any relationship will find the information within this book very insightful and encouraging.

What I've lost is irreplaceable—my wife, my church, and nearly my sanity. God has a unique way of selecting which individual He calls to suffer, but normally it is twofold: to impact the life of the one selected and to impact the lives of those they influence. I wasn't selected because of any infidelity, abuse, or neglect; I was simply called to suffer many things for God's name's sake.

My degree of pain was unfathomable, and yet I realize that "My Pain" was for "Your Gain"!

Chapter 1

DISORDERLY CONDUCT

Looking back, I often wondered why, throughout my life, I could only achieve a limited amount of success. I had lived my entire life as a person who did just enough to give off the impression of being a successful individual. I called this pattern of illusion the "D Syndrome," for if I got a "D" as my final grade, then it would be enough for me to pass the class. In grade school I did just enough to achieve the minimal passing grades for the academic completion of mandated courses. Middle school and high school were followed by the same inner-behavioral actions, which allowed me to graduate high school by the skin of my teeth. My reading, writing, and math skill levels were very poor and below the standard for a high school graduate. But somehow, I graduated high school with my diploma in hand. And I did it all by believing in the "D Syndrome."

I remember shortly after graduation, my mother asking me if I wanted to be the first member of our family to attend college. She was willing to make the personal sacrifice if I made the choice to venture college, but I told her that I was not interested in going. By now, the pattern of doing just enough to get by had become woven into the fabric of my mind. Not seeing this as a habitual problem, I continued to make bad choices that I convinced myself were good choices.

Getting jobs after high school was not a problem for me, because I was very personable. Having a good appearance and mannerisms got me into the doors of many employers but keeping me there and excelling throughout the company was a totally different story. I never took advantage of the opportunities several of my employers gave me to further my education, which undoubtedly would have resulted in professional growth, as well as promotional opportunities. Instead, throughout my career I remained comfortable working in entry-level positions that did not present opportunities for real growth.

Fear was not the culprit in my limited success, nor was it the lack of the presence of promotional opportunities. It was something internal that I was not aware of at the time. Most of the time, I would make decisions after reacting to a situation, instead of making my decisions based on deep thought and contemplation. The theory that any action is considered progress has been my method of operation for as long as I can remember. It had become a way of living for me even after I became a Christian.

Christianity, for me, was accepting a new way of living by no longer thinking carnally but thinking spiritually. I convinced myself that God was in complete control of my life, and all I had to do was follow His leading. Twenty-eight years later, the pattern of doing just enough to get by had never been unwound and was still tightly woven into the fabric of my mind. Addressing the deeply rooted issues of my past had now become the topic of discussion for my personal development. The current condition of my mind would not allow me to research all the events that I had gone through during my lifetime. So, I narrowed the parameters of my research to only remembering those events that happened after I became a Christian.

Although I've had the privilege of learning from many individuals (both good and bad), I could never seem to maximize my potential of becoming truly successful. No matter what ventures I undertook or the goals that I had set out to achieve, I would, for the most part, end up with minimal success. I had grown accustomed to operating spontaneously without the proper planning, placing all the eggs of reasoning into one basket, relying on the profits from great ideas prior to the implementation of those ideas, and not adequately preparing for the worst-case scenarios. These methods of operating were still the norm for me, and I had become blind to the need for change. Because I am gifted in many areas, I could not see that most of the challenges that I faced were not because of outside influences, but rather came from inner issues that I was unaware of.

I did research on a medical condition called Attention Deficit Hyperactivity Disorder (ADHD), which is when a person has differences in brain development and brain activity that affect attention, the ability to sit still, and self-control. At times, everyone struggles to pay attention, listen and follow directions, sit still, or wait their turn. But for people with ADHD, the struggles are harder and happen more often.

I've learned that people with ADHD may have signs from one, two, or possibly all three of the following categories:

- **Inattentive** – People who are inattentive (easily distracted) have trouble focusing their attention, concentrating, and staying on task. They may not listen well to directions, may miss important details, and may not finish what they start. They may daydream too much, seem absent-minded or forgetful, and lose track of their things.

- **Hyperactive** – People who are hyperactive are fidgety, restless, and easily bored. They may have trouble sitting still or staying quiet when needed. They may rush through things and make careless mistakes. Without

4

meaning to, they act in ways that they shouldn't and may act in ways that disrupt others.

- **Impulsive** – People who are impulsive act too quickly before thinking. They often interrupt, aggressively seek or take, and find it very hard to wait. They may do things without asking permission or act in ways that are risky. They may have emotional reactions that seem too intense for the situation.

When I read over the signs of a person with ADHD, I immediately knew that I had a problem. My behavioral patterns throughout my life were a definite indication of possible ADHD. Although I would not admit it right away and I quickly shrugged it off as just a coincidence, I now had to be honest with myself and embrace this possibility. I see now that I've always had inner issues that have gone unrecognized and unaddressed for years. Most of my struggles have been as a direct result of my inner issues, and not from any outside influence.

I have been taught biblical truths, practical living, and religious traditions by some of the most adept spiritual leaders of my day, but somehow, I have found it easier to fashion those teachings into what I thought they meant. What seemed arrogance or pride to many people was in all actuality an unknown mental disorder. I was labelled a rogue—hard-headed, strong-willed, and downright stupid at times because of the disorder. Yet God for His name's sake kept me covered through it all.

Timing is everything with God, and as a Christian, I often wondered why God did not just cure me from this disorder right away. It would have spared me a lot of embarrassing moments and brought Him much more glory, but God knew that I needed to stay in that state for as long as it took. Many people could recognize that I had a problem, yet I was the only one who needed to see that I in fact had a problem. Many have tried to speak on the obvious issues that I was facing, only to be rejected or blown off for being non-supportive of what I felt God was directing me to do. It was very easy for me to see the problems that resided in others, but very difficult for me to see those personal problems that were operating within me.

My definition of success was not based on fame or fortune. Rather, it was based on how much glory God would receive as a result of my actions. I believed that I was not consistent enough regarding success, and the pain of failure had become increasingly harder for me to bear. Limited success for me had become the norm, so much so that I would water down any extraordinary vision, idea, goal, and/or plan from God that involved me. So, I gave in to my shortcomings by identifying them as just part of my character, never seeing them as a possible cause of my demise. God allowed me to go through this inner struggle for over fifty years, and one day, I found myself on my Damascus road.

The Damascus road experience that I'm referencing was revealed through the life of the biblical character Saul of Tarsus (later known as the apostle Paul), found in the book of the Acts of the Apostles.

> *And Saul, yet breathing out threatenings and slaughter against the disciples of the Lord, went unto the high priest, And desired of him letters to Damascus to the synagogues, that if he found any of this way, whether they were men or women, he might bring them bound unto Jerusalem. And as he journeyed, he came near Damascus: and suddenly there shined round about him a light from heaven: And he fell to the earth, and heard a voice saying unto him, Saul, Saul, why persecutest thou me? And he said, Who art thou, Lord? And the Lord said, I am Jesus whom thou persecutest: it is hard for thee to kick against the pricks. And he trembling and astonished said, Lord, what wilt thou have me to do? And the Lord said unto him, Arise, and go into the city, and it shall be told thee what thou must do.*
>
> *Acts 9:1-6*

Like Saul, I've chosen to go through life doing what I felt was right, only to find out that what I felt was right was actually wrong. I dealt with the vicissitudes of life as I saw them, only to discover that I had been blind to the truth. To God, this was the perfect time for me to finally see the error of my ways, and it had to be done in divine fashion. Getting my undivided attention required a miraculous chain of events. My internal issues had become so imbedded within me that one miraculous event would not be enough to really get my attention.

God used ten plagues to get the attention of the children of Israel when they were slaves in Egypt. This miraculous chain of events was the very thing that they needed to break through the many layers of mental, physical, and spiritual challenges that they had experienced. The more complex the issue, the more compound the remedy. The events of the ten plagues had become the light that shone into the eyes of the children of Israel, exposing their internal flaws. Internal issues are devastating, and they can in fact hinder people from reaching their maximum level of success. When internal issues are revealed unto a person, it is up to that person to make the necessary changes. Sometimes it doesn't matter how many miraculous events God chooses to use to get one's attention, ultimately, the individual must choose to make the change. Choosing to change is never easy, but take it from me, it sure is worth it!

My internal issues were many, so one miraculous event might not have brought them all to the surface. Sometimes the most effective treatment for an individual who suffers with multiple issues is to remove all the issues at the same time. God knows what He must do and how He must do it to get the proper response out of me. I understand that God loves all His children, but He doesn't treat everyone the same. My issues may not be your issues, and your issues may not be mine; so, there are times when God must deal with us individually.

How God got my attention was very simple: He removed those things that I loved the most. The Bible teaches that God is a jealous God, but what He had to do with me was not an act of jealousy; rather, it was out of necessity. What He allowed to happen with my marriage and with the church where I pastored was very drastic. My marriage of twenty-three years ended in divorce, and after fifteen years as pastor, the church where I served was now defunct. I had become damaged beyond repair. I went into seclusion, while being swallowed up in guilt and shame. It seemed to me there was no way I could face the world after getting divorced and losing the church. My life at the time (in my eyes) had reached a massive degree of failure.

Too many things were happening at the same time, and I knew this could not just be a coincidence. I believed God was trying to get my attention for whatever reason, and I had become determined to find out why. After months of blaming others for the current misfortunes that plagued my life, I soon realized that nothing could happen to me unless God wanted it to happen or permitted it to happen. So, I soon had to look at myself both psychologically and spiritually, and that was when I first began to see my inner flaws being revealed. For many years, the signs of a person diagnosed with Attention Deficit Hyperactivity Disorder had mirrored most of my actions down to the letter. I cannot medically diagnose myself as having ADHD, but the symptoms were too real for me to ignore.

As a Christian, it is my responsibility to examine myself frequently. While examining myself, I saw that *inattentively*, I have always had trouble—focusing my attention on one thing, concentrating, and staying on task. I don't listen well when complete instructions are given, frequently missing out on important details, and at times I don't finish what I started. I saw that *hyperactively*, I have always been restless. I find it difficult to stay still or stay quiet when needed, I often rush through things and make careless mistakes, and at times I may act in ways that disrupt others. And I saw that *impulsively*, I would at times act too quickly before thinking things through. I found it difficult at times to wait on things, I often did things without asking for permission, I sometimes acted in ways that were risky, and I was prone to have emotional reactions that seemed too intense for the situation. These flaws were hindering me from maximizing my level of true success, and I desperately needed to do something about it!

To me, success can only be defined when I reach that level of glory that God desires from me at any given moment. God was not getting much glory out of my life at that time, and He allowed me to see it as well. After seeing the error of my ways (both hidden and seen), I earnestly fell on my face and repented to God for my actions. Then I made a vow to Him, a vow that I was going to see through, for this vow was not like any other vow that I had made to God. This time, I had a clear understanding of my internal struggles and what I needed to do for the cycle to be broken. Turning from my wicked ways would not be easy, but with the help of God and with a renewed mind, all things could become possible! If words were indeed spiritual, then I must be very careful not to speak negative things into existence. I did not have ADHD, but the similarities regarding its symptoms prompted me to make some much-needed changes in my life.

Although the change came in my life after fifty years of living, I am grateful to God for proving His grace throughout the entire time that I had disorderly conduct. I know now that the process of my acknowledgement of the disorder and the way that God chose to cleanse me from the disorder were nothing short of a miracle. Even though the entire process was very painful, I fully understand that **"my pain"** was indeed for **"your gain"**!

Chapter 2

A FATHER'S IMAGE

Allow me to digress within this chapter and take you back to my early childhood. I was about four years old when I saw the image that changed my life forever. I was the fifth child out of seven, and the youngest boy, which entitled me to be known as "Mom's baby boy." I was known to cleave very closely to my mother and would often cry when she was not in my line of sight. Some would call me spoiled, while my mom would just say, "That's my baby boy." Legend has it that one day, while sitting in my highchair, I was crying profusely, for no other reason but to just get attention, and I fell out of the highchair and hit my head hard on the floor. After that devastating fall, my mother described that experience as the fall that cured my disease of crying all the time for no reason.

It was not the experience of falling out of my highchair that broke my habit of crying all the time. Rather, it was being traumatized after witnessing my father brutally beat my mother in our kitchen. At the age of four years old, I was traumatized into becoming a bitter, angry, and vengeful child. I wanted nothing more than to kill my father for his cowardly acts that he had been inflicting upon my mother for years. I became consumed with hatred for my father, and I was not smart enough to hide my feelings. I wore that desire on my sleeve every chance I got. I no longer responded to life as a normal child—no more crying, no more longing for affection, no more laughing and healthy communication. A dark cloud had permanently covered my dreams of having a normal life, all because of the image of my father abusing my mother.

My father's image would become the basis upon which all my life decisions were made. It was tragic to have my childhood consumed with such hatred, inasmuch that I could never enjoy the benefits of a natural childhood. Growing up with my father's brutal image in my head had robbed me of any sense of normalcy and caused me to make some bad decisions throughout my life. In 2011, I watched an amazing movie entitled *Columbiana*, starring Zoe Saldana. This movie had me in tears because it depicted the resilience of a child who set out to avenge her parents' deaths at the hands of a known drug overlord. Although it took the child over twenty years to avenge her parents' deaths, she remained focused on the pain, which proved to be her source of guidance throughout her entire life. I could empathize with the nature of her vindictive character, because I too had undergone a similar pain that was driving me.

Finding relief from traumatic pain can sometimes be very difficult. My mind had become manipulated into believing that my actions toward my father were justified, and those privileged persons with whom I secretively shared my pain did nothing more than co-sign my delusions of grandeur. I know now that hatred in any form is wrong, yet that level of trauma had turned my heart wicked and clouded my mind, making me feel justified. Although the thoughts of murdering my father crossed my mind for years, they soon faded as I gain more knowledge about the legal penalties. So, I had to find another way to inflict pain on my father for all the pain that he had inflicted upon my mother.

My mother eventually left my father, with her six children, and moved to Washington, DC. She started a relationship with an old friend named Joe Joseph. Mr. Joe was a nice man who never physically harmed my mother (as far as I could see), and together they had a seventh child to add to the bunch. Having a new baby sister was quite a joy, and we were seemingly on the right path to becoming a healthy family once and for all. But after several years, something went wrong in their relationship, and Mr. Joe left, leaving my mother with the responsibility of now raising seven children on her own. The flames of anger in my father's image were now fanned by the vicissitudes of life, and I was back on the warpath of vengeance. But I never faulted Mr. Joe for anything that was evolving in our lives, for I believed that the foundation of all our troubles began through my abusive father. So, my father's image continued to haunt me.

I heard someone say, "Success is the best way to get back at your enemies." I realized that I could possibly go to jail for inflicting any physical harm on my father, so I decided to become successful in the areas where he had failed as a man. The phrase, "I'm doing this because I don't want to be like my father," had become the foundation for my personal achievements. It was a negative motivation of epic proportion, yet it pushed me further along in my quest to become successful. Achieving success by way of normal channels such as hard work, diligence, prudence, and skillful planning was not my method of operation. Everything I did in life was based on me not ending up like my father. The image that was driving me was spawned from me witnessing my father beating my mother in our kitchen at an early age.

I became domestic because I didn't want to be like my father. I never saw my father lend a hand to help my mother as she struggled to raise her children. As I grew, I would cling to my mother as she went about doing her motherly duties. I watched her for years, a degraded, torn-down woman who sacrificed herself for her children. During those times of observation, I learned how to cook, sew, wash and iron clothes, clean a house, and perform minor repairs. My domestic skills did not come from any home economics class in school but came from watching my mom as she nurtured her children and honored her role as a wife to an abusive husband.

What I learned from my mom would later help me to be at the top of my game, when it came to me being independent. I did not want to become a man who thought that it was the woman's job to do all the work in the house, and his job was simply to pay the household bills. What I had learned from my mother would prove to be valuable assets for building a healthy home in a family-oriented environment. I remember in junior high school, when I invited my female friends over to my house, how they marveled at the fact that I knew how to cook and do the household chores. Undoubtedly, this made me very popular—not just with the girls I invited over, but with their parents as well, because those girls could not wait to share that key information with their parents. Achieving those simple abilities had become a notch on my personal belt, because this was something my father never achieved. So, I did those things because I never saw my father do them.

I never knew if my father was educated or not, because all I ever knew him to be was a truck driver. Being educated was not a prerequisite for the job at the time. So, I wanted to be smarter than my father by graduating high school and getting a good job to support my family. My next goal was to help my mom financially. Seeing how she struggled even while receiving government assistance was disheartening to me. I remember watching my mother apply herself at the right time in her life and receive a good paying job at a big company. A few years later, she lost that job and was forced to go back to living on government assistance. Although I wanted nothing more than to help my mother financially, I soon realized that good paying jobs were not given to those with just a high school diploma and no technical skills.

Searching for that pie in the sky was like hitting the Powerball lottery. The odds were stacked against me because I was an inner-city child with a limited education. So, I moved on to the next goal of achieving something that my father never did, and that was to gain personal wealth. I started making money on the streets selling drugs, hoping to one day hit it big like some of my neighborhood friends who became local dealers. Never achieving prominent status, I remained a low-level drug dealer, barely making $100 per day. Always just doing enough to get by and never surpassing my goals, I found myself becoming more frustrated than profitable.

I believed that any change was progress, so I moved out of my mother's house to become independent. After high school, I was working in low-level jobs at various companies while selling drugs after hours. I began making about

$3,000 per week and became consumed by the drug culture and lifestyle. I quickly forgot why I got into the game in the first place. It was supposed to be to help my mother become financially stable. It became more about helping me instead of helping her, but I soon found out that money, power, and respect gained through the streets are very short-lived. Soon I began using drugs and making some very bad decisions in life. Some of those bad decisions caused me to lose all my material gains, and I ended up facing time in prison. It was then I realized the street life was not for me, and I had to find another way to continue my plan for vengeance toward my father.

I became a Christian in 1990, yet my father's image had remained woven into the fabric of my mind. You would think that by now I would have left that type of thinking behind, especially after becoming a new creature in Christ. Although I was now a Christian, I continued to operate in the same methods of old, possibly because I wrongfully believed I was now doing everything in the name of Jesus.

It's very easy for me to overlook an internal issue, especially if God doesn't point it out to me. The problem that I encountered was that even though I had changed spiritually, I still struggled emotionally with some deeply rooted issues. At the time, I could not see the imminent danger, because I couldn't sense the urgent need for a much-needed transformation.

I see now that when I gave my life to Christ in 1990, I had developed two natures, which the Bible calls "the old man and the new creature." I was too blinded by my inner issues, so I could not see the importance for me to address the old nature, for my newfound nature is spiritual and is governed by the principles outlined in God's Word. My old nature is carnal and is governed by me, by way of my emotions, intellect, and heart. I was more pragmatic in my actions and less focused on being led by the Spirit of God. This was the great divide that had fueled the constant battles between my flesh and my mind.

My father's image in my past was still strong in my mind and very influential in making key decisions. I got married because I wanted to prove that I wasn't going to be an abusive husband like my father. I was a paragon as a provider for my family because I didn't want to be absent like my father, and I did many other things because I didn't want to be like my father. Allowing myself to be guided by my father's image had robbed me of the natural order of things. Operating out of fear of failure was easy for me, but I missed out on the richness of doing things simply out of my love for them.

I had no clue as to where this fear of failure came from, yet it became clear that it was indeed self-inflicted. No one told me that I would end up like my father, nor is it found in my genes that I would end up like him, but for whatever reason, I took that burden upon myself. The natural order of things would be to operate in love, yet to operate in fear increases the abandonment of the true nature of personal achievement. I rarely felt the fullness of personal achievement because of my misguided reasons for its pursuit.

The Bible informs us that we are spiritually made in our heavenly Father's image and in His likeness, yet ironically, it was an image of my earthly father that at times hindered me from reflecting the image of my heavenly Father in the sight of people. I had no clue just how misguided I was even after becoming a Christian, because I continued to operate in the same mindset of my past. Although Christ had freed me after my confession of faith, I remained a slave to some critical issues from my past.

Deeply rooted issues often go unnoticed, and they have a way of becoming a natural part of one's life. God ultimately determines when to expose those hidden issues, and often at a time we can't anticipate. The pain caused by the image of my father abusing my mother had become a permanent fixture in my mind, and I had grown so accustomed to it that it didn't hurt anymore. Negative images that you have become accustomed to are the most dangerous, for the heart can influence the mind into believing that the negative image is somehow justified.

> *"With the mind I myself serve the law of God; but with the flesh the law of sin."*
>
> *Romans 7:25*

The contrast between my mind and my heart can be very complex and it often leaves me halted between two options. Do I do what God says? Or do I do what my heart says? It is very difficult for the mind to win the battle over the flesh when the flesh has gained strength from a traumatic image. That image is constantly being rewound and played back within the mind, making the thought of deleting that image more difficult with every repetition. The more an image is rehearsed in the mind, the more relevant it becomes to the heart.

The human mind is very complex because it has a myriad of parts, making it almost impossible for any person to completely rely on it for guidance. Transformation of the mind is the only solution to prevent the inevitable letdown of putting trust in our finite minds. Adopting the same mindset that Christ Jesus had is key to making Godly decisions. Now I see that carrying my father's image in my mind for over fifty years has played an intricate role in why God could only receive limited glory from my life. God required more of His glory to be poured out of me, so He had to create a process of deleting that image from my mind. The process of deletion was not without a cost. It was very painful, because I would have to suffer great loss. But I can honestly say that **"my pain"** was for **"your gain"**!

Chapter 3

CALLED TO SUFFER

Throughout my life, I would often find myself in painful situations. In most of them, I would focus on the "how" of the pain (how much it hurts) instead of the "why" of the pain (why this happened). I do not like to suffer, but I had to learn that suffering has always been a part of God's divine process for my life. Through much prayer, fasting, and the reading of God's Word, I discovered that I was in fact "called to suffer" … and suffer many things throughout my life I did.

> *"The steps of a good man are ordered by the LORD: and he delighteth in his way"*
> *Psalm 37:23*

As a Christian and a follower of Jesus (who is the Christ), I have come to believe that my life is not my own. I unequivocally believe that every step I have made in my life has been either "ordered" or "allowed" to happen by God. I believe that nothing happens in my life without God's approval, and I was selected by Him to be used exclusively for His glory. The challenge that I faced after I gave my life to God was not serving Him but trying to understand His reasoning behind the steps that I had taken (especially the painful steps).

Giving my life to God was my last resort, for in my mind, it was the only option I had left after trying everything else. I had spent the first half of my life doing what I wanted to do and how I wanted to do it. It wasn't until I found myself at a critical point in my life (which I called the end of the road) that I accepted Jesus (who is the Christ) as my personal Savior and Lord. Now my life is forever being transformed by God into the man that He desires me to be.

Twenty-five years after I gave my life to God, I found myself once again at the end of the road. With the loss of my marriage of twenty-three years and with the loss of the church where I served as pastor for fifteen years, I had become bitter, confused, and angry with God. I became withdrawn from everyone because I could not understand why God would allow these things to happen to me.

I did not understand, because since I gave my life to God on March 7, 1990, I never took my life back from Him. In fact, I was completely committed to whatever He had planned for my life. I lived holy (set apart from worldly living). I served faithfully at church. I was a faithful husband to my wife. I had become a paragon regarding provision for my family. I did the very best that I could for fifteen years as the pastor of the Revelation Center, Incorporated, and I helped those within the communities in which I travelled. I just couldn't understand why God would allow this to happen to me!

It was the blow I didn't see coming that knocked me down to the ground, and that was when my emotions found a way to take over my mind. I could not fathom living without Stacey (my wife of twenty-three years and the mother of my three children) and the fact that I could no longer effectively shepherd the members at the Revelation Center, Incorporated. So, I hid myself in a symbolic cave, hoping to remain secluded from the rest of the world. While in this symbolic cave, I found myself engaged in many conversations with depression, suicide, murder, shame, guilt, anger, loneliness, and heartache. Those feelings would often find ways into my mind and hold meaningless conversations with me, but thanks to the Spirit of God who lives within me, those negative feelings were not allowed to stay for any long periods of time.

In 2017, I found myself resting at the Church of New Hope and Faith, Incorporated, under the leadership of Bishop James McNeal, Jr. In New Hope, Bishop McNeal taught me a valuable lesson, for he taught me that when it comes to my obedience to God, "understanding was not required." That was the beginning of many profound lessons that the Bishop taught me during my tenure at the Church of New Hope and Faith.

For years as a Christian, I fooled myself into thinking that I would always be comfortable with God's plan for my life. But in my heart, I would only be comfortable if God's plans were compatible with *my* plans. I even found scripture to support my carnal thinking:

> *"Delight thyself also in the LORD: and he shall give thee the desires of thine heart."*
>
> *Psalm 37:4*

Because of the emotional pain that I was enduring, I wanted God (for just this once) to let my will be done instead of His will. I quickly gave up my way of thinking and accepted the fact that I was chosen by God to suffer for such a time as this! So, I began to think about the words of Jesus when He said, "Not my will, but Thine Will be done" (Luke 22:42).

God loved me enough to indulge me by revealing His plan for my life and the reason for the pain I was going through. He told me (through Scripture) that like the apostle Paul, I was also a chosen vessel unto Him, to bear His name before the strangers, the officials, and the church, "For I will show him how great things he must suffer for my name's sake" (Acts 9:16).

Accepting what God had allowed to happen had proven to be very difficult at first, but the more I gave Him the reins in my life, the easier the process of suffering became. I became proactive and took ownership of my personal faults, while looking at my difficult situations not as problems, but as tools God was using to create a better me. I needed (for God's sake) to become a better person, a better husband, and a better pastor, so He could maximize the level of glory that would be produced out of my life.

The journey would not be easy, but it would be worth it. Some days the pain would be easier to handle, but some days I would find myself losing that day's battle. I knew I needed to obtain spiritual balance in my life, and nothing calms a wayward spirit like the Word of God. I had to find supportive scriptures to help soothe my wounded spirit, and there were many biblical characters from whom I could draw strength, because they too were called to suffer. I first found myself intrigued by Job:

> *There was a man in the land of Uz, whose name was Job; and that man was perfect and upright, and one that feared God, and eschewed evil. And the LORD said unto Satan, Hast thou considered my servant Job, that there is none like him in the earth, a perfect and an upright man,*

one that feareth God, and escheweth evil? Then Satan answered the LORD, and said, Doth Job fear God for nought? Hast not thou made an hedge about him, and about his house, and about all that he hath on every side? thou hast blessed the work of his hands, and his substance is increased in the land. But put forth thine hand now, and touch all that he hath, and he will curse thee to thy face. And the LORD said unto Satan, Behold, all that he hath is in thy power; only upon himself put not forth thine hand. So, Satan went forth from the presence of the LORD.

Job 1:1, 8-12

Although the story of Job was an excellent reference regarding suffering for God, it was not the right example for me because Job and I were not from the same background. Job was perfect and upright, a man who feared God and stayed away from evil. On the other hand, while growing up on the mean streets of southeast Washington, DC, I was neither perfect nor upright. I was drawn to doing evil things, plus I did not even know God at that point of my life. So, I kept searching the Scriptures and found the story of the prophet Hosea:

The beginning of the word of the LORD by Hosea.
And the LORD said to Hosea, Go, take unto thee a
wife of whoredoms and children of whoredoms:
for the land hath committed great whoredom,
departing from the LORD.

Hosea 1:2

Like Hosea, I was very committed to God as a servant, but God never asked me to marry a whore. My wife, Stacey, had never slept with a man before she met me, and to my knowledge, she never had an affair during our twenty-three years of marriage. So, I could not relate to this story, and I was forced to keep searching the Scriptures until I found the story of the apostle Paul:

And there was a certain disciple at Damascus,
named Ananias; and to him said the Lord in
a vision, Ananias. And he said, Behold, I am
here, Lord. And the Lord said unto him, Arise,
and go into the street which is called Straight,
and enquire in the house of Judas for one called
Saul, of Tarsus: for, behold, he prayeth, And hath
seen in a vision a man named Ananias coming
in, and putting his hand on him, that he might
receive his sight. Then Ananias answered, Lord,

*I have heard by many of this man, how much evil he hath done to thy saints at Jerusalem: And here he hath authority from the chief priests to bind all that call on thy name. But the Lord said unto him, Go thy way: for he is a chosen vessel unto me, to bear my name before the Gentiles, and kings, and the children of Israel: For I will shew him **how great things he must suffer** for my name's sake.*

Acts 9:10-16

The scriptures that I found associated with the life of the apostle Paul were more relevant to the circumstances that involved my life. Like Paul, I had a very difficult upbringing, and I was forced to do whatever I thought I needed to do to survive. With seven children and one parent, my family was poor, so we had to learn how to adapt to the harsh living conditions that came with it. My father was physically abusive toward my mother, so much so that she had to flee our home in Philadelphia and move to Washington, D C, for the safety of her children.

Drugs and crime plagued our neighborhood, and I quickly become a product of my environment. It was not long before I gave in to the pressure of living in poverty, and I began selling drugs while in high school. I found myself incarcerated for the first time at the age of fifteen, facing sixty years in prison, and in my twenties, I started committing crimes and ultimately became addicted to drugs. Eventually I was captured by the law, and subsequently held in prison because I could not afford to post bail. During the nine months I was held in prison, I first heard the voice of God.

The voice told me that I belonged to Him, and that I had been given one final chance to live a changed life. I had exhausted all other options for how to live my life, and I was headed toward a certain death. At the age of twenty-four, while sitting in that jail cell, I took God up on His offer. I told Him yes and asked Him what He wanted me to do. God told me to leave Washington, D C, and head back to my birthplace in Philadelphia. My uncle Lawrence Simpson allowed me to stay in his home under one condition, and that was that I would really be serious about getting myself together.

I knew there was nothing in my past to go back to, so I pressed forward to see what God had planned for me. On March 7, 1990, I found myself in church at the Christian Tabernacle COGIC (Church of God in Christ), where I accepted Jesus (who is the Christ) as my personal Lord and Savior. It was there that I gained the knowledge of God, under the leadership of Rubin T. Jones, Jr., who gave me my spiritual foundation. This helped me to develop a meaningful relationship with

God. I realized very early that I was happy as a Christian and that my life had changed for the better.

Like the apostle Paul on the Damascus road, I had a profound spiritual encounter with God during my last incarceration. Although there were many lessons for me to learn regarding this new Christian lifestyle, one thing was certain: I was not going back from whence I came. Twenty-eight years after I got saved, I am finally convinced that I was indeed "called to suffer" by God! And this degree of suffering was not unto death. Rather, it was for the glory of God, that the Son of God might be glorified thereby. It is good to know that **"my pain"** was for **"your gain"**!

Chapter 4

SELF-INFLICTED RESPONSIBILITY

My life is not my own, because I surrendered it unto God when I became a Christian. The concept, through my religious belief, is to submit to God as the supreme authority and guidance over my life. Yielding total control unto God was very difficult in the beginning, because I had no clue that I needed to develop a deeper relationship with Him first. I found myself surrendering my life to God, only to take it back from Him whenever I came across situations that I believed I could handle myself. This give-and-take mentality was not spiritually healthy, because it never rendered God total control over my life. Subsequently, God became secondary in my life, as opposed to Him being primary, as my beliefs suggested.

A surrender is often viewed as a negative action, but when you are willing to surrender to God's authority, it becomes an act of servanthood through gratefulness. My struggle is like most people, I have a very difficult time with the word *surrender*. To me, the word *surrender* was not a "you do, or you don't" word. I chose ignorantly to gage it through a percentage format. I believed as a Christian that I only had to surrender unto God at least 60 percent of the time. Most of us don't even recognize that we do this because it happens so often, and it has grown into a customary way of living for the Christian believer. For years I've sung the old hymn of the church, *I Surrender All,* not understanding the true meaning of the word *surrender.*

Not only did I allow God's position as Lord over my life to fluctuate, I even chose the moments of subjugation that I would render unto His authority. Any other leader would have viewed this type of conduct by his subjects as an act of rebellion, which would by law constitute some form of punishment. But because of His grace and mercy, God would often turn away His judgment and wrath. Looking back, I don't even know why I'm still alive after all that I have done against God, not to mention all the things that I have done to other people. Yet, God remains faithful and patient toward me, for I guess He knows I will eventually get myself together.

You would think that after becoming a Christian, it would have been easy for me to give my all to God, but the truth of the matter is that it has been very difficult. I see now that most of my struggles were within me, and oftentimes, I didn't even know I had a problem, because I could only see what was in front of me. The wars going on beneath the surface of my skin

were corroding the very fabric of my character and relationship with God. I often wondered how those problems got into
my heart, mind, and soul in the first place.

If you neglect the purpose of something long enough, you
will ultimately forget that it even has a purpose. God gave
me five senses, which enable me to smell, taste, touch, hear,
and see. Every one of those five senses have the propensity
of becoming a portal for discovery of my environment. I can
smell saltwater before I reach the ocean, taste items to see if
they are safe prior to consumption, touch an object to gage
its temperature, hear a siren before the arrival of an emer-
gency vehicle, and see a storm brewing from several miles
away. These senses allow signals to be sent to my brain for
assessment and help me to calculate an appropriate response.
Although I'm grateful to be blessed with these faculties, I
know now that I can't totally rely on them when making life
decisions.

Case in point: the eyes are one of several portals by which
external things (both good and bad) can enter the mind. Seeing
things through my own eyes can be very challenging, because
there is a propensity for me to make choices based only on
my observation of an object. I've been blessed by God to
have been created with beautiful hazel eyes that sporadi-
cally change colors. This has always been an attraction for
most females, but even beautiful eyes with adequate vision

aren't always reliable when it comes down to making proper judgments.

Our vision can be skewed at times, hindering our ability to make accurate assessments of what we see. Physical sight can be minuscule compared to spiritual insight, for spiritual insight comes directly from the eyes of God. It is always better to seek God's vision of a thing, instead of relying on what is seen through our own eyes. God is omniscient and omni-present, so there is nothing that He doesn't know or hasn't seen. Yet, I tend to trust in what is seen through my eyes, instead of relying on how something is seen through God's eyes.

The mind can be easily swayed by the heart (that is, our flesh), and when information is gathered through the portal of the eyes, the heart instantly decides whether it's going to sup-port the mind or go against it. There were times when I saw something that I knew wasn't right according to God's stan-dards, but my heart convinced my mind to try it out anyway. Subsequently, I found out that because I looked at something for too long, my heart became inquisitive. When my heart becomes inquisitive, it begins to rationalize the cravings for what it desires instead of what God says. Here I am a born again Christian, with a heart that constantly tries to rationalize how to make something that is wrong seem right.

Adam and Eve took of the forbidden fruit, even though they had been given a commandment not to touch the tree.

God gave the command before the forbidden act, and their downfall was "self-inflicted" because they allowed the wrong information to enter their hearts (via their five senses). The command was given unto them by God to not touch a specific tree in a specific location. It was their job to protect their obedience to that command and keep at bay anything that would lead to a contradiction. God will always have an adversary, with the sole purpose of creating situations of contradiction for God's people.

The adversary does not have the power or the ability to mount a successful campaign directly against God, so it attacks God through the children He loves. To get the children of God to self-inflict their downfall with an act of disobedience has always been the ultimate goal of the adversary. The methods of infiltration are vast, yet the purpose remains constant: "Get the children of God to change their minds." The quickest way into the mind is through the portals of the senses. Protecting one's obedience to God is very complex and requires a constant mental focus on what God said. An adversary is a shapeshifter, which can become a person, a thing, an idea or an action. The origin of the adversary can be either internal or external, for the conflict can just come from within me without any outside influence.

I had to remember that nothing can happen to me as a child of God that hasn't already happened to someone else. I used to think that my personal issues and circumstances were unique, but I soon found out that I'm not the first person, nor will I be the last person, to go through difficult times. I allowed my senses to be the portal through which the adversary would enter, and that was when the war between my heart and my mind began. Condemnation would be the normal posture after a lost battle, because it never allowed me to review the actions that led to the loss as a preventive measure. Guilt and shame would hinder my chances of gaining the proper knowledge and understanding that would better position me for victory for the next battle. My guilt and shame would lead me to try to forget what happened, instead of proactively reflecting on what happened.

I would often gain the strength to face my personal challenges when I searched the Scriptures and found another child of God with a similar experience. Adam and Eve were given a commandment from God, not to touch a tree located in the middle of the garden. While alone in the garden, the adversary approached Eve with a simple conversation, which became the beginning of a series of unfortunate events. Eve was bombarded with an onslaught of information that proved to be too much for her to properly process. The information gained access into Eve's heart by way of her senses. Eve's heart became overwhelmed as vast information came through the various portals of her senses. *Listening* to the serpent, *looking* at the tree, ***touching*** the fruit of the tree, ***tasting*** the fruit, and giving it to her husband led to the most catastrophic event that ever happened to mankind.

> *Wherefore, as by one man sin entered into the world, and death by sin; and so death passed upon all men, for that all have sinned.*
>
> *Romans 5:5*

Our senses (hearing, sight, touch, taste, and smell) can be a direct point of access into our heart, causing it at times to contradict what God has said. I see now, like Eve (in the book of Genesis), I too had allowed external information and internal emotions to gain access to my heart, creating times when my heart would war against my mind. "Create in me a clean heart, O God; and renew a right spirit within me". *(Psalm 51:10)* denotes the need for a continual cleansing of the heart, for me to maintain a right spirit. To maintain a right spirit, I have to constantly have my heart cleansed, to ensure that I retain a healthy relationship with God.

The first Sunday of July in the year 2003 is where I would like to begin my story concerning "self-inflicted responsibility." The prior Saturday, I was officiating at a funeral service at the Kimble Funeral Home. A young man approached me after the service. This young man proceeded to tell me how much he and his family enjoyed my sermon, and they wanted to know if I was available to minister at their church tomorrow. At that time, my calendar was open, and I told them that I would gladly come to their church to minister.

When I first began preaching at Revelation Baptist Church of God, I was a guest preacher because they had no pastor at the time. The Lord was with me, and my gift of preaching, teaching, and singing went over well with the congregation. At the conclusion of the service, they asked if I would be willing to come back next week as well. Several weeks turned into several months, and the congregation soon asked if I would be willing to become their new pastor. Our relationship was at its genesis, therefore, I suggested that we allow at least one year to pass before we held a vote on the matter.

As the newly appointed interim pastor, I learned that this church was comprised of several families who were some years ago members of the Wynnfield Baptist Church. The families had decided to leave Wynnfield Baptist because they could no longer maintain a healthy relationship with pastor. The members of these families came together in 1994 and formed the Revelation Baptist Church of God. They formed a search committee, designed to find pastoral candidates who would be a good fit for their newly founded organization. Nine years later, they had experienced at least five different pastors, and once again, the pastoral seat had become vacant. Most people would say that this was a difficult group of people to lead, but their philosophy was simple: we (the members) are going to run our church, and the pastor's job would just be to preach and teach.

Having no idea of what I was getting into, I was one of several ministers who held the position of pastor at this church, and I had to learn their method of operation the hard way. This would be a huge step for me at the time, because I was used to faithfully serving at my former churches as an active elder. I was not in training to become a pastor at the time, but I must admit that the opportunity was very flattering to my ego. The members knew exactly what to say initially and how to respond to me appropriately. The plan was for me to be the interim pastor for one year, then hold a special meeting where the members of the church would elect or reject me as their new pastor.

While preaching at the church during the first couple of months, my emotions were overwhelmed with a self-perceived responsibility of becoming a pastor. I believed that God had just given me a baby in the form of this church, and I would be expected to personally take care of it and its members. Of course, no one told that to me, nor was it divinely spoken by God, yet that internal emotional idea would become the origin of the years of my "self-inflicted responsibility."

Because I was not yet fully committed to God, I became a vulnerable individual operating in the position of pastor. I felt it was my responsibility to maximize the potential of this struggling congregation, inasmuch that I was willing to do anything for its survival. Most of the time, my thought process had come from the "image of my father," for I was still driven by the notion that I needed to succeed, out of a fear of failure. I became an easy target for the adversary and easily swayed by my inner struggles. Information from sources other than God had gained access to my heart through the portals of my five senses.

I *saw* the personal struggles of some of the members, I *listened* to the advice of other people, I *tasted* the false power associated with being a pastor, I *touched* the lives of many people, and I *smelled* the aroma of future achievements. I would often allow outside information to find its way into my heart through the portals of my five senses. Although I loved God with all my heart, I still allowed my emotions to take control at some of the most crucial times.

As the interim pastor, I observed a lot about the church, and I saw that it was desperately in need of change. The way in which they operated as a church was a bit archaic, compared to the progressive style of operation that I had grown accustomed to. Most of the changes I had suggested, based on how the church operated, were received with inspiration and excitement. But change had become very difficult for those who were in authority, and before the "year of getting to know one another" was complete, I found myself with opposition coming from some of the church leaders. Ultimately, I was asked by the church leadership (by way of an official letter), to vacate my position as their interim pastor.

What the leadership did not understand at the time was that the language outlined in their bylaws and constitution required a special voting session on the matter by its current members. By that time, the church had grown to twice as many members, and the majority of the membership was now on my side. I was voted in as the newly appointed pastor, and those who were in opposition simply faded away over time. This was in no way a personal victory for me, for I had grown very fond of all the members, especially the original founding families.

As time went on, I began to reorganize how the church operated, but first we had to rewrite the church bylaws and constitution. God had called me to lead this church as a pastor, not as a hired minister who was just paid to preach and teach. Changing the way that the church had been governed was the key to me exercising my authority as pastor, for the current laws had given that power solely to the executive committee, and most of these individuals were no longer members of the church. God knew the original founders formed this church out of rebellion, and He had sent me there to break up that type of foundation.

> *And every one that heareth these sayings of mine, and doeth them not, shall be likened unto a foolish man, which built his house upon the sand: And the rain descended, and the floods came, and the winds blew, and beat upon that house; and it fell: and great was the fall of it.*
>
> *Matthew 7:26-27*

Many changes had come to the Revelation Baptist Church of God since my arrival in July of 2003. The fluctuations over the years regarding church growth, method of operation, partnerships, church vision, financial status, community outreach, etc., were like a revolving door. Because I was not being completely led by God, I would often find myself taking one step forward while taking two steps backward. All the difficult times that I had faced as the leader of this church were, without question, because of **"self-inflicted responsibility."** Had I listened to God more and to myself less, things would have gone in a very different way. But God knew that for me to get the help I really needed, He would have to bring this chapter of my life to a close.

The Revelation Center (formally known as the Revelation Baptist Church of God) was defunct in July of 2018, exactly fifteen years after I became the minister and final pastor. Looking back, I see now that God had covered me with His grace throughout my tenure. The number five represents the number of God's grace, and the number three represents the number of the Holy Trinity (God the Father, God the Son, and God the Holy Spirit). I would not have made it fifteen years without the grace of God, for even with my flawed character, God saw fit to see me through it all.

There is not enough room within this chapter for me to detail all the events that took place during the fifteen years I held the position as pastor. I could write an entire book on the highs and lows of pastoring a church, especially regarding those who are first-time pastors. The main thing I struggled with from the very beginning was how to keep myself and my inner struggles out of God's way. People will always have personal struggles and limited skill sets, but a good pastor must learn how to love them through it all. The soul of every person must be more important to a pastor than their membership, their money, and their degree of service to the ministry. Pastors should first and foremost be in this business for the purpose of saving souls, not for the large membership or any personal achievements.

Information that does not come directly from God can often make you confused and unclear of what God said. The goal of the adversary has always been to find a way to cause us to harm ourselves regarding our obedience to God. I harmed myself by allowing my emotions and the lack of understanding be my guide in most situations as the pastor of the Revelation Center. It was never my responsibility to take care of God's church, for that responsibility had only been given to His Son, Jesus (who is the Christ). The years of "self-inflicted responsibility" caused much pain and devastating lost to many people. Yet, if I had to do it all over again, I would do it, simply because **"my pain"** was for **"your gain"**!

Chapter 5

A DOOMED MARRIAGE

*And the L*ORD *God said, It is not good that the man should be alone; I will make him **an help meet** for him. And the L*ORD *God caused a deep sleep to fall upon Adam, and he slept: and he took one of his ribs, and closed up the flesh instead thereof; And the rib, which the L*ORD *God had taken from man, made he a woman, and brought her unto the man. And Adam said, This is now bone of my bones, and flesh of my flesh: she shall be called Woman, because she was taken out of Man. Therefore shall a man leave his father and his mother, and shall cleave unto his wife: and they shall be one flesh. And they were both naked, the man and his wife, and were not ashamed.*

Genesis 2:18, 21-25

Marriage is a union created by God, designed to give an individual companionship and support. The innate desire to share one's life moves an individual toward a relationship. Relationships are quite different from friendships, for friendships are general while relationships are internal and personal. Relationships are unique in their own nature, and no two relationships are the same.

The inevitable problem comes when an individual uses a method of operation from other relationships that they have either seen, read about, or heard of. We often find it easier to mimic another person's relationship, instead of pursuing the uniqueness of our own personal relationship. This mindset has proven to be destined for failure, because it often causes the abortion of the natural evolution and uniqueness of our own personal relationship.

Everyone wants to be in a unique relationship, but the fear of the unknown (or should I say, the fear of the discovery) can easily tempt a person to mimic other relationships. From the beginning of creation until this very day, we all have either seen, heard, read, or fantasized about other relationships. To mimic a relationship is a humanistic device that is seen as a part of our normal behavior, but it is nothing more than a coping mechanism. Information concerning the relational behaviors of other people (whether their relationships were good or bad) can find its way into our hearts through the portals of our five senses and become the driving force behind our relational journey.

As for me, my father's abusive relationship with my mother became the driving force behind my relational journey. The obsession of not wanting to be like my father was overwhelming, and I was convinced that this feeling was justified because of the resounding pain that it caused me. The problem with my thinking regarding my relationships was that I operated out of the fear of failure instead of operating out of the joy of discovery through a unique experience. The fear of failure was indeed self-inflicted, for no one told me I would end up like my father. The fear of not becoming like him became the foundation for my reasoning regarding future relationships.

The relationships that I ventured into during the first half of my life were very selective, and I was committed to the other person for as long as the relationship lasted. Marriage was not a part of the equation at the time, because it was not a necessity, as far as I was concerned. It wasn't until I became a Christian that marriage became a thought-provoking issue. I had not been taught the biblical purpose regarding the principles of marriage, therefore, I engaged in relationships based on those that I had witnessed growing up. I was never one to mimic or fashion myself after someone else's relationship, mainly because there were no relationships within my bloodline that I felt were worthy of emulating. So, the pain of my father's relationship with my mother had become the foundation on which the building blocks of my personal relationships were built.

I know now what I did not know then! My marriage was doomed from the beginning, simply because I allowed my relationships to be guided by the pains of my past. If the main reason for me getting involved in a relationship was spawned out of the fear of failure, then ultimately, I would miss the true purpose and principle of marriage. The beauty that could have been seen through the scriptural evolution of two people becoming one flesh never came into its fullness because of a gross misconception. In ignorance, I thought the biblical statement, *And the two became one flesh,* simply meant my future wife would assume my last name and become an extension of who I was.

That misconception had guided my thought process, even after I gave my life to God. It was like "the blind leading the blind," for I was blind because of my scriptural ignorance and led by the blinding pain of my past. The lack of biblical understanding coupled with a wounded spirit ultimately became what doomed my marriage. Because of the pain my father had inflicted upon my mother, my heart had become tainted and my mind was fixed, and I swore I would never become like my father. I did not become consumed by this self-inflicted passion to never become like my father to impress other people. Rather, it was an inner-self achievement that I believed could one day heal me! For even though my reasoning to pursue marriage was wrong, it felt justified because I wanted nothing more than for the pain of my past to stop.

I remember in 1990 when I came back to Philadelphia from Washington, DC, in search of a new life, my uncle Lawrence Simpson took a chance on me by letting me stay at his home with his family. He had a wonderful mother-in-law named Dorothy Jones, and she invited me to visit her church. She impressed upon me to leave my old nature behind and not to start out my new lease on life by seeing how many girls within the church I could possibly develop relationships with. Dorothy Jones planted the seed of marriage in my heart by telling me not to go around dating different girls, but to find one specific girl within the church I could court with the intention of someday marrying. What Dorothy Jones didn't know was that I had already succumbed to the pain of my past, and I wanted nothing more than to be married. My only goal at the time was to be successful in every area where my father had failed.

From the first time I laid my eyes on Stacey, I knew she was the one who would become my wife. Although I was twenty-five years old and she was only nineteen, it felt very natural that our paths would cross at that time. The phrase "opposites attract" was an understatement, to say the least, for I was a derelict from the inner city, and she was the product of a religious household with strong family values. A few years later, we were married, and soon after that, we started our own family. I set out to become a great provider for my family, which was something my father had failed to do for us. Making sure my wife and children were provided for was something of a priority for me, and some days would prove to be harder to manage than other days.

I took my primary role as the provider for my family very seriously, and I did whatever I had to do to make sure my family would never be without the essentials of life. Stacey would do everything she could to lend a helping hand, whenever times got too hard for me to handle alone, but her primary role as a mother was to nurture our children. God's favor was upon my life, and by His grace and mercy, my family has always been provided for. Achieving the status of being a great provider for my family was self-fulfilling, because it was something my father did not do for us.

Being guided by the pains of my past had blinded me to what was most important, for all I could think about was being a great provider for my family. The position of being a "good husband for my wife," on the other hand, would never receive the proper cultivation, because I was so focused on being a "a good provider." My priorities were out of whack because of the fear of failure, and I allowed what was of the least importance in life to overshadow what was of the most importance. When it came down to my family, being a good provider seemed easier for me to accomplish than becoming a good husband. To me, my father was neither a good husband nor a good father, and that left me as a young man on the road of life without a role model and without the proper guidance. So, in regard to my priorities, the role of being the provider had taken precedence over the role of being the husband.

I could never put as much thought into becoming a good husband because that facet of my life required intimacy. I had never had an intimate relationship with anyone (including family and friends), because growing up in a hostile environment caused me to become more of an introvert (a shy, reticent person). The pains of my past began at an early age and provoked me to become reticent (not readily revealing my thoughts or feelings). Therefore, most of the difficulties that I faced growing up, I held within and found them very uncomfortable to discuss openly. Women assume every man knows about intimacy, but I never learned what true intimacy was because I associated it with sexual engagement.

It's easier for people to revert to what is comfortable and familiar, rather than to face the uncertainty of a challenge. Hiding the fact that I was unlearned in a particular area had become almost second nature for me. I was too ashamed to admit that I didn't know something and hiding that fact had become a terminal illness. Instead, acquiring the much-needed knowledge regarding those areas of lack, guilt and shame got the best of me. Deflection from the things that I was not good at, became the first option in response to what I wanted people to notice about me. My perceived learning disorder prevented me from achieving knowledge beyond my personal experiences, to the point where maximizing my true potential seemed unreachable.

After our children had come of age and were able to make conscious decisions on their own, things began to change within our marriage for the worse. Stacey would often make gestures, and sometimes statements, about how she wanted me to become more intimate with her without sexual engagement. Of course, I had no clue what she was talking about, and I would shrug it off as another silly complaint. I would often feel unappreciated as a husband, for all that I had achieved for my family. I felt she was becoming tremendously ungrateful, because I was doing everything I could as the provider for my family. Achievements for the family through personal goals was my focus, while intimacy through communication was what she longed for the most. As a mother, she felt very satisfied because of all the sacrifices she had made for the sake of the children, but as a woman, she would often be left feeling empty.

We were raised on different sides of the tracks, and it seemed as though we could never find a way to fuse both worlds. In my world, I thought the responsibility of taking care of the family ultimately fell on the shoulders of the man. I believed that after all involved parties (my wife and children) had shared their opinions about any household issue, at the end of the day, the final decision would fall on me.

Making the hard decisions regarding my family was never easy for me, because I'm not a man who believes "it's either my way or the highway." I was so afraid of dropping "the ball of responsibility" by not making the final decisions, I would become stressed out or fall into a depression. I couldn't see myself telling God, "Hey, it wasn't me who made that decision, it was that woman you gave me!" So, I firmly believed that after all the information and suggestions were gathered and placed on the table of life, I had to now make the very hard choice of selecting what I thought was best for the entire family. Stacey could never embrace the fact that I really believed the full weight of my decisions was in fact my curse. I was terrified to make a final decision yet horrified to leave that responsibility up to someone else.

No matter how difficult the process of decision making was for me internally as the head of my household, my wife would always conclude that "he doesn't listen to anybody but himself!" That was very painful for me to hear, mainly because I only heard it spoken whenever I made a final decision that was different from her decision. Some of the decisions that I've made over the years have been directly linked to her insight and passion on a subject, but I can't remember a time when she said, "My God, he does listen to me after all." She told me she had reached a point in her life where she didn't need me to make any decisions for her. She believed that if her decision was different from mine, then no final decision should be made at all, if the outcome was ever going to gain her support.

The truth of the matter was, we never took the time to put in the effort to work together as a team, and the two never learned how to become one! Because we were both raised from different sides of the tracks of life, we never saw the importance of each other's personal experiences, so the word "Compromise" was seldom used within our marriage. That would prove to be a major roadblock toward our marital success. As Christians, we both were very religious and established among our peers as preachers of the gospel. When needed, we each knew how to find specific scriptures to support our personal viewpoints during any disagreement.

It became a constant battle as time went on, because we really didn't know how to communicate our differences clearly with each other. Disagreements turned into disconnection, and disconnection turned into sporadic moments of distance, all because of the lack of understanding regarding the word *compromise*. I never knew that I couldn't have a truly committed marriage without compromise. I thought that if two people loved each other and were committed to the responsibilities that came with marriage, then that would be enough for a strong and lasting marriage. There are basically two reasons why people compromise: one is when you fully trust the other person, and the other is when you fully rely on the other person.

I never needed my wife to accomplish anything for our family, because I had "the fear of failure" to do that. The fear of turning out like my father would be the driving force behind all that I did. I made sure my family would always have a roof over their heads, they would always have clothes on their backs, they would always have food on the table, they would always be safe, and (frequently) they would always enjoy the finer things in life! All those things were accomplished with very little help from my wife, simply because I believed it was solely my responsibility to do so! It was not because she didn't want to help me, but I really believed she shouldn't have to, because that was my responsibility!

I had grown accustomed to being a great provider for my family and being a social leader to those whom I served in the community. Life experiences and wise counsel from a myriad of individuals over the years have helped shape me into a strong-willed person. And as a strong-willed person, I became very defensive toward any opposing opinions regarding my actions. I welcomed any opinion concerning my actions, as long as it was delivered through healthy communication. But when a person tried to communicate their opinion about me in a negative way, then I would instantly become offended and would often disregard what they had to say, even if what they were saying was right. I believe it takes a lot of effort and patience for a person to *convince me* of their opposing opinion, then it would take a person who went *against me* in a flippant or disrespectful manner, just to get their opposing opinion heard.

As time went on in our marriage, my wife became increasingly comfortable in voicing her personal opinions regarding my life choices, and it seemed as though we never learned how to agree to disagree. We never knew how to work together as a team, so consequently, we would often clash as two individuals who happened to be married.

After our children were on their individual journeys toward adulthood (via their four-year collegiate experiences), my wife began her quest to find her identity as a woman. Meeting me at the age of nineteen, getting married at the age of twenty-three, and starting motherhood at the age of twenty-five seemed to have left her with a void regarding the experience of becoming a woman. One's personal identity can often go unseen when they are connected to someone else, especially when the two individuals don't know how to spiritually operate as one.

Being married to a person of vision can be very challenging, especially if they are seemingly in the vanguard of all they are involved in. My wife had always felt as though she was in the shadow of a husband with a personality that stood out front on most occasions. Being in the shadows is rarely seen as a good place, because it can be hard for anyone to see their strengths after being in such a position. Stacey now longed to step out of my shadows and walk independently as an independent woman of God.

A profound nurturer never desires to be seen while they are in operation; rather, it is hoped that the fruits of their labor are seen through those whom they have nurtured. My wife is a paragon of motherhood when it comes to our children, and working in the shadows was never an issue before. When her maternal skillset was no longer needed as a priority for our children, she began her quest to come out of the shadows. She started to realize that she was just as important as her husband, just as gifted as her husband, just as knowledgeable as her husband, just as valuable as her husband, and just as spiritual as her husband.

Companions had now become competitors, for we no longer compromised on family issues; rather, we seemingly competed on every level. The foundation of our marriage had now become lost in the maze of life, simply because we both were caught in the web of selfish desires. Wanting things to stay the same as they had been throughout our marriage was undoubtedly a critical error on my part. Desperately wanting things to change personally, but not knowing how to make those specific changes, would prove to be the error of her ways as well.

Our marriage was doomed to fail, mainly because we both had some personal issues that were deeply rooted in our pasts, and we both omitted dealing with them prior to getting married. Omitting an internal problem is worse than committing an external problem, because it renders your mate clueless to your personal issues and prevents them from being helpful to you at the most critical of times. We had never known the internal struggles of each other's past, because it wasn't something that either of us felt comfortable talking about to each other. So, when dealing with predominant issues were omitted, they would often lie dormant in our hearts and at times produce volcanic eruptions full of untamed emotions. Confrontation now took the place of communication, because what had not been spoken for years now chose to speak. It's hard to suddenly articulate what has been silent for years, because it might just be a past issue that has become a relic, instead of being a part of a relevant conversation.

The lack of communication between my wife and me had become the norm, and our marriage was failing because of it. Unjustified pride mixed with guilt, hurt, feelings of betrayal, shame, and feelings of abandonment had clotted our hearts for years. We found it to be easier to avoid talking about our deeply rooted personal issues, rather than to continuously enter in an argumentative pattern of communication. A man and a woman who never knew how to properly deal with their internal flaws were destined to become emotionally unraveled at the marital seams.

We concealed our individual flaws for years, until they could no longer be hidden, and one day, we both awakened unto "**a doomed marriage**." Losing my marriage to Stacey was the most painful experience that I had ever undergone, but now I see that **"my pain"** was for **"your gain"**!

Chapter 6

MIRRORED PAINTINGS

*Why is light given to a man whose way is hid, and whom God hath hedged in? For my sighing cometh before I eat, and my roarings are poured out like the waters. For **the thing which I greatly feared is come upon me**, and **that which I was afraid of is come unto me**. I was not in safety, neither had I rest, neither was I quiet; yet trouble came.*

Job 3:23-26

Our beliefs are our own, and though they may originate from many different sources, at the end of the day, it is our beliefs that do in fact shape how we respond to adversity. It is not the circumstance that dictates our response; rather, it's our belief about the circumstance that guides our response. No one puts a gun to our heads or pushes a button in our brains to make us respond to adversity. We are in complete control of how we respond to adversity. Our beliefs are deeply rooted, and they shape the way we respond to adversity. Most people find it easier to blame others for their response to circumstances, never accepting the reality that it was their beliefs about the circumstances that caused them to respond as they did. Adversity is a part of the natural order in life, but our belief about the adversity can either lead to our success or our failure.

An artistic license is granted to anyone who dares to capture their own personal views on the canvas called life. Every painting that has ever been painted was created through the eyes of an artist. The details of each painting are unique, simply because the artists captured what was seen through their own eyes and described on canvas what it meant to them. The metaphor "the canvas called life" means that a painting could be perceived in many ways by the audience, but it only expresses how things are seen through the eyes of the artist. A painting is not a mirror, for it is designed to show the story behind the artist and not the story behind the viewer. For whatever reason, people love to create "mirrored paintings," because most of the time it supports what is already in the mind of the viewer. Deeply rooted beliefs that are not open for change can lead to the creation of "mirrored paintings." When a person with deeply rooted issues looks at a painting that reminds them of a prior experience, they often turn a simple painting into a personal mirror. This is the basis of the old Chinese proverb: *What the eye sees and what the ear hears, was already in the mind.*

I spoke in the prior chapter about "a doomed marriage," but what I would like to share now is that its destruction did not happen overnight. My wife and I were both blinded for years by our own internal issues. We struggled with things such as deeply rooted beliefs, undisclosed personal issues, pride, guilt, shame, and a lack of understanding toward one another. Ten years prior to getting a divorce, we were like two ships passing each other on the sea called marriage. We stayed together for the children and for the image of a Christian married couple and never seemed to care enough about ourselves as two emotionally damaged individuals.

Two hours per day of recreational time in the yard for a prisoner is not true freedom, but it's "an illusion of freedom." Although the prisoners are still incarcerated, they have grown accustomed to "illusional freedom" because the mindset of most prisoners has become "some freedom is better than no freedom"! For years, my wife and I participated in "illusional freedom" within our marriage, even though we both were still bound by the strongholds of our past.

Then said Jesus to those Jews which believed
on him, if ye continue in my word, then are ye
my disciples indeed; And ye shall know the
truth, and the truth shall make you free. If the
Son therefore shall make you free, ye shall be
free indeed.

John 8:31-32, 36

As Christians, we both believed every word of the Bible, but I've found out that we both had the propensity of releasing things within us that had been spiritually bounded by God. The more distant we became from each other, the stronger the chances were of those personal issues becoming freed. When emotional upheaval reached its boiling point within our marriage, those deeply rooted personal issues resurfaced with a vengeance. No matter how committed we lived our lives to God, there would always be some personal issue that would test our spiritual commitment.

Coming from a broken home, living in poverty, raised in underserved communities, engaged in a life of crime, enduring drug addiction, and being undereducated were the roots of my personal strongholds. Most of those strongholds were broken immediately after I accepted Jesus (who is the Christ) as my Lord and Savior on March 7, 1990. Although I still struggled with the image of my father, as stated in Chapter 2, I continued to testify regularly about all that God had delivered me from. Because I was new to the church and had a dysfunctional past, I was often wrongfully labeled as a wolf in sheep's clothing by the religious community. It is hard for people to believe in a person they don't really know, so I was often misunderstood and ostracized by many; yet, I remained faithful to God and to my wife and family.

It was not a shock to me that over the years, people would assume that our troubled marriage was a result of my troubled past, and the first thing people wanted to know was, "What did he do to mess up the marriage?" The first thought regarding a broken marriage (in the eyes of the general public) has always been, "It must have been the man's fault," and it's widely assumed that he had to have committed an unspeakable act that caused the divorce. I knew that, for the most part, I would get the blame. Little did everyone know, for a long time I felt responsible for her actions as well as my own actions.

Over the last thirteen years, we have seen at least eight different marriage counselors, and most of these counselors were pleasantly surprised that I was not involved in any infidelity, physical abuse, or drug or alcohol addiction, nor did I father any children outside of our marriage!

It was revealed during those counseling sessions that I was indeed a great father to our children and an awesome provider for the entire family, but I ended up becoming a lousy husband who took too many risks at home and within the ministry where we served as pastors. She had expressed, candidly, that as a woman, she was getting older and her desires had become more of a priority at this point in her life. At the end of the day, she had lost confidence in me as her husband and as a spiritual leader, to the point that she did not feel safe as my wife.

Years of counseling cannot change a person when a person's mind is already made up. What was never revealed in any session during those years of marriage counseling was that my wife had created "mirrored paintings" that made it extremely difficult for her to stay married to me. Every one of the marriage counselors believed our troubles could be worked out, because we were both good people who really loved God. But when there is a strong desire, fueled by traumatic images of the past, it can lead a person to push even God to the side.

Stacey came from a very strict Christian family, where she grew up in church and developed a strong relationship with God at an early age. She was considered by most to be a model Christian, who on the surface did everything right in the eyes of people, by which she gained much respect and admiration. The life that she now lived (spiritually and naturally) had become a life of torment, for she was constantly engaged in spiritual warfare. She was beginning to unravel as her mind became captivated by some strong images from her past. This person who had become such an inspiration to many was in fact suffering in silence as her flesh warred against her mind.

My wife had developed a strong prayer life and had become an awesome preacher and teacher of the Word of God. To the public, her life reflected everything she believed, which in turn revealed the strength of her relationship with God. However, the level of our relationship with God is completely dependent on our responses — and how we respond to God is how He measures our love toward Him.

> *And why call ye me, Lord, Lord, and do not the things which I say?*
>
> *Luke 6:46*

Our behavioral response to what God speaks directly to us is often driven by an image in our mind, and it's our belief about the image that will determine if we are going to comply or disobey. During a time of adversity, we often fail to correctly respond to the voice of God, for the battle between our heart and our mind usually follows. Psychologically, three variables impact how we respond to God's voice during a time of adversity: (1) being able to predict, (2) maintaining a sense of control, and (3) maintaining a sense of optimism. If during a crisis you don't have a solid grip on predictability, control, and optimism, then you will become unraveled at the seams.

Mental images are never true reflections of reality. They are nothing more than abstractions of what we think may happen next. Mental images are shaped by our beliefs, our value systems, and our past experiences. No two people share the exact same life experiences, nor do they share the exact same beliefs and values. How our brains work is that we tend to respond to patterns. A current image can be placed within the context of an older image. Once we believe what the image is to be, then we revert to a familiar template, to which we respond consistent with that image.

There are many sources from which our beliefs originate: there are hand-me-down beliefs, cultural beliefs, religious beliefs, and advertised beliefs. No two people share the same beliefs, and our beliefs are so different that there is a propensity for two people to hear contrasting information from the exact same words. Our beliefs, our values, and our past experiences help shape the image in our minds and ultimately govern our responses.

We all have been guilty of allowing what we believed about an image in our mind to override our inner voice of reason, sound advice from wise counsel, and at times even the divine voice of Almighty God. We all have sinned or do in fact make mistakes, but God often elects to respond to our trespasses on an individual basis. Biblically speaking, everyone in the Garden of Eden ignored the divine voice of

God and responded contrary to what He said. At this junc-
ture, God chose to deal with all of the involved parties on an
individual basis:

> ¹⁴ *And the* LORD *God said* **unto the serpent**,
> *Because thou hast done this, thou art cursed*
> *above all cattle, and above every beast of the*
> *field; upon thy belly shalt thou go, and dust*
> *shalt thou eat all the days of thy life:*¹⁵ *And I will*
> *put enmity between thee and the woman, and*
> *between thy seed and her seed; it shall bruise*
> *thy head, and thou shalt bruise his heel.*

> ¹⁶ **Unto the woman** *he said, I will greatly mul-*
> *tiply thy sorrow and thy conception; in sorrow*
> *thou shalt bring forth children; and thy desire*
> *shall be to thy husband, and he shall rule*
> *over thee.*

> ¹⁷ **And unto Adam** *he said, Because thou hast*
> *hearkened unto the voice of thy wife, and hast*
> *eaten of the tree, of which I commanded thee,*
> *saying, Thou shalt not eat of it: cursed is the*
> *ground for thy sake; in sorrow shalt thou eat*
> *of it all the days of thy life;*¹⁸ *Thorns also and*

thistles shall it bring forth to thee; and thou
shalt eat the herb of the field;[19] In the sweat of
thy face shalt thou eat bread, till thou return
unto the ground; for out of it wast thou taken:
for dust thou art, and unto dust shalt thou return.

Genesis 3:14-19

Although I was not given a divine pass from the things that I had done wrong throughout our marriage, God chose to deal with my wife and me on an individual basis. I remember God speaking to me in 2017, saying, "**Guard your heart**, for what happens next is permissive!" I had no clue what God was referring to, for He was willing to give us grace instead of destruction, by the implementation of "our will" as oppose to "His will."

It had become evident in 2016 that God had grown tired of both of us, as we insisted on having things our way instead of yielding to what He was saying. God began to orchestrate a series of unfortunate events that would shake us at our very core. Like Adam and Eve in the beginning, God dealt with my wife and me individually and responded independently to our insubordination. God was breaking us both down simultaneously, yet in very different fashions. I will discuss in detail in the next chapter what events God used to break my stubborn will.

I remember in 2016 that Stacey was involved in **six car accidents** within the same year, and although some of them were minor fender benders, a few of them were life threatening. Each time she had a car accident, God revealed that she was about to cause a spiritual wreck in her life. Sometimes God attempts to get our attention through catastrophic events that are designed to draw us nearer to His presence and enable us to hear His voice with more clarity.

God loved Stacey too much (and those who happened to be passengers during those six car accidents) to allow any devastation to fall upon her, for no matter what He said or revealed unto my wife, her mind was already made up that she was going to leave me. God never once told my wife to leave me. My wife would often say to me, "God didn't tell me to leave you, but He doesn't want me to live in pain either."

There are times in our lives that no matter what God speaks to us, we are going to do whatever we feel we must do to survive. We all process pain differently, but when we focus on the effects of the pain more than the purpose of the pain, we often make the wrong decision to seek relief instead of revelation. Sometimes during times of calamity, God does not respond favorably to our prayer requests, and because of the pain, we misinterpret any action as progress.

In 2016, while in our final marriage counseling session with Vincent Calloway, she made a startling statement, and I quote: "I'm already gone, but I'm trying not to be." She had become angry, bitter, impatient, and stubborn, to the point that she just wanted relief from the emotional torment that had consumed her. At this point in our marriage, it didn't matter what I did to make amends; her heart was fixed, and her mind was made up. She was resolved to do what she had seen others do in her past, as opposed to what God told her to do.

What blindsided me was that I only knew Stacey as a living example of a strong mother for our children and a strong Christian woman, regarding her personal relationship with God. I had no idea as to the degree of the battles that were raging within this anointed woman of God! She struggled with images that dated back to her early years as a child, images that would prove to be detrimental during her later years. Although an image is not the cause of our negative response to God, our belief about the image keeps us from maximizing our godly potential.

Later in our marriage (when the children were in their teens), things got very dark for us individually, and our marital relationship began to decline. Stacey would reveal to me toward the end of our marriage, "I have to apologize to you because I only did what I knew!" What I didn't know was that she was tormented daily by how our marriage had turned out, because it reminded her of the images in her mind of her parents' marital relationship. Instead of just looking at her parents' life as a learning tool, she embraced it as an image of what our marriage would become. That is what I call turning a painting into a mirror, thus the term, **"Painted Mirrors"**!

The thing that hurt the most was that we were both model Christians who worked diligently for the sake of the church, and yet we didn't work diligently for the sake of the marriage. Stacey had become ashamed, because our marriage reminded her of her parents' marriage. She strongly believed there was an uncanny resemblance regarding how her parents' relationship ended up and where our relationship had gone.

She believed most of the time during her parents' marriage that her father made her mother feel undervalued and insignificant. Intimacy and romance were not prevalent for years between her parents, and that model marriage was actually dysfunctional behind closed doors. Her father had become narcissistic, while the raw beauty of her mother became corroded through bitterness. The image of their broken marriage would forever remain in the mind of Stacey, to the point that she made a vow to never allow that experience to happen to her. The mental painting from the negative images of her past had somehow been transformed into a mirror. What Stacey feared the most in life had seemingly come upon us as she gazed mentally into that "painted mirror."

*Why is light given to a man whose way is hid, and whom God hath hedged in? For my sighing cometh before I eat, and my roarings are poured out like the waters. **For the thing which I greatly feared is come upon me**, and **that which I was afraid of is come unto me**. I was not in safety, neither had I rest, neither was I quiet; yet trouble came.*

Job 3:23-26

Toward the latter part of our marriage (mostly during emotional upheaval), Stacey started noticing some similarities between our responses and those of her parents. We would have disagreements that turned into silence, and that silence would last for various lengths of time. We would become two ships living in one house, purposely passing each other while avoiding any unnecessary interaction. Because of the lack of intimacy, instances of sex were few and far between, and we had developed meaningless routines as parents instead of a healthy relationship as a married couple.

My wife looked at a painted image of her parents' marriage and turned it into a mirror that gave a reflection of how she believed our marriage would turn out. Although I was not aware of the details nor the depth of pain that the image of her parents' marriage played on her mind, I still believed we were not them, and God could still fix anything that was broken within our marriage if we both believed that our marriage could be saved.

Finding a way out of our marriage was very difficult for Stacey, because she could not find a valid biblical reason to justify her claim. For I was a great father to our children, I was a great provider for our family, I wasn't caught in any extra-marital affair, I had not fathered any children outside the marriage, I wasn't physically abusive, I wasn't drug- or alcohol-addicted, and I wasn't a convicted criminal. It was hard for her to find the justification and support for leaving. It turned out that I just wasn't the kind of husband she had imagined or desired me to be.

Because I embraced the roles of being the priest of my home and the senior pastor at the church, I would often feel the extreme burden of responsibility as the person at the helm of it all. I had no experience in true marital partnership, because Stacey and I never could seem to operate on the same page. We played our roles as individuals on team Stanton but never seemed to move as two who became one. Even as the clouds of uncertainty arose within our marriage, I remained hopeful that God could fix it.

The self-inflicted responsibility of making choices that involved others became overwhelming for me, for I believed that *at the end of the day, I would be the one held responsible by God for everything that happened, both in my home and at the church, whether good or bad!* Regarding my family and the church, I didn't always make the best choices, and I may not have done everything morally acceptable by many people, but I did the very best that I could with what I had.

My wife had begun judging me more on my mistakes than she would on my accomplishments. The internal wars going on inside of me at the time were increasing, and the pressure of it all had pushed me closer to the edge insanity. I loved Stacey more than anyone in this world, and she was the only person I really needed to talk me off that edge. When it became evident that she had turned against me, the light of hope was dashed from my heart. I didn't believe that I could have done so much wrong that it caused her to leave me, and to this day I'm still devastated by her response.

I remember some of the profound statements made by a few of the marriage counselors we visited, that after listening to my wife's argument during our sessions. They said to her, "Why are you so judgmental toward your husband?" and "Why do you harbor so much animosity and anger toward your husband?" It was not customary for a Christian wife to harbor such negative feelings toward her husband. Some of the marriage counselors did admonish my wife to continue to pray for her husband, for they believed God would honor her prayers and works out anything that was wrong with my character.

They told her to just be patient, because they believed God would change me for the better in the process of time.

Over the years, Stacey had developed an incomparable relationship with one of the women of the church, and unknown to me, this relationship proved to be detrimental to our marriage. For this person had a kindred spirit with my wife, and they had so much in common that they became inseparable as spiritual sisters. Her spiritual sister was involved in her own broken marriage at that time, in which she and her husband lived separate lives under the same roof. Very few people knew they had been separated for years, while living under the same roof. They believed their marital circumstances were personal, and they should not let it interfere with how they served in ministry.

This type of marital resolution has been going on within the religious community for as long as anyone can remember, and it seems to have become the normal for our culture as well. The topics of separation and divorce are rarely discussed in religious institutions, because of the frequency of occurrences amongst its leaders. Instead of addressing the issue as an epidemic, it is viewed as an embarrassment and normally swept under the religious rug. Generation after generation, the religious community has endured immeasurable marital breakups, and yet there has not been a clarion call for concern. That may be why the religious community holds the highest rate of divorce and separation amongst any other group or demographic.

I was never interested in knowing how other Christian marriages were faring until my marriage became troubled. Then one day, I took a personal survey on the condition of one hundred Christian marriages. These were couples I had personally known since 1990, and to my surprise, the results were devastating. I know that all married couples go through a variety of problems, and I'm not being judgmental, but numbers are irrefutable. Out of the one hundred Christian marriages that I surveyed, a staggering 63 percent of them were either divorced, separated, or remarried! The struggle is real regarding marriages, but if we as Christians continue to sweep our marital struggles under the rug, the cycle will continue for the next generation.

For my wife, the picture of her spiritual sister's marriage had turned into a mirror, and it gave off a false reflection of what our marriage was to become. So, it seemed that separation was the way out that she had been looking for. Stacey found the support for her emotional condition when she embraced her spiritual sister and possibly other Christian marriages that had participated in similar methods of resolution. But once again, I stated to my wife that we were not them and they were not us, for I still believed that God could fix anything that was broken within our marriage.

Stacey revealed to me that at an early age, she was exposed to some sexually explicit content on television. This content sparked a strong interest in intimate relationships. A developing fascination for intimate relationships had ensued, and she began reading romance novels that were sensual at an early age. Images would be forever etched in her mind, and they became the foundation of her desires. When difficulties hit us in real life, we often resort back to a fantasy hidden within the images of our minds. If we are not careful, the image can become a refuge during times of struggle, and the fantasy can in fact take the place of reality.

When you tend to look at your life through a mental picture, by changing a painting into a mirror, you allow that picture to reflect how you would like your life to be. It can become frustrating for anyone who realizes, "How I feel about my reality does not compare to how I feel about my fantasy." Emotions that have become unraveled during a time of marital upheaval could lead one to gravitate towards *a want* instead of *a need*. My wife discovered that she wrestled constantly with *the image of what she wanted* against *the man God knew she needed*. It is very dangerous for us to allow our personal wants to override what God decided we needed. For He did promise to provide all of our *need*, according to His riches in glory, and not just those things that we *want*.

Although I was the only man my wife had ever known sexually, I've come to find out I was not the only man she had ever known intimately. As Christians, we are taught through the Word of God to guard the very thoughts of our minds, because our thoughts have the propensity of becoming images. Images can become very enticing, and if we're not careful, we can find ourselves wanting to be more involved with an image than what is real.

> *Rejoice in the Lord always: and again I say, Rejoice. Let your moderation be known unto all men. The Lord is at hand. Be careful for nothing; but in every thing by prayer and supplication with thanksgiving let your requests be made known unto God. And the peace of God, which passeth all understanding, shall keep your hearts and minds through Christ Jesus. Finally, brethren, whatsoever things are true, whatsoever things are honest, whatsoever things are just, whatsoever things are pure, whatsoever things are lovely, whatsoever things are of good report; if there be any virtue, and if there be any praise, **think on these things**. Those things, which ye have both **learned**, and*

*received, and **heard**, and **seen** in me, do: and
the God of peace shall be with you.*

Philippians 4:4-9

We all can be misled by our own scriptural interpretations, especially if our interpretations agree with our fleshly desires. The Bible is very clear when it denounces all forms of sexual impurity and fantasies that would involve adulterous relationships, whether actual or mental. Sexual impurity and fantasies can become habit-forming and addictive. Men and women often engage in pornography and other adulterous fantasies to reach a sexual climax. Having a poor sex drive within a marriage is often not the real problem or issue. Most breakdowns in marital relationships comes through the lack of understanding regarding the role of sex in a marriage. Sex was designed as an action that not only gives pleasure but expresses love, unity, and commitment to each other. Intimacy and sexual pleasure are very hard to find when there is a noticeable lack of an expression of love, unity, trust, and commitment in a relationship.

My problem throughout our entire marriage has always been my focus on what made me a great provider for my wife and family. I grew up thinking that making provision for my family was the highest form of love that I could ever show them. God blessed me to be a great provider, for they always had shelter, clothing, food, needed material things, and vacations and travels, and could participate in events that most people could only imagine. In my ignorance, I had worked unselfishly for years, providing what Stacey needed as a wife, but I lost sight of what she needed as a *woman*.

I began to think toward the end of our marriage that she had become very ungrateful, judgmental, and non-supportive. The feeling of being betrayed by my wife had blindsided me. I was in so much psychological pain that I became an introvert and less communicative during the latter part of our marriage. Had the betrayal come from the hands of anyone else in the world, I could have taken it better, but it came from the very person I loved the most! For years, I was damaged beyond human repair, yet I remained a great provider, for that was the responsibility God gave me. Providing what I thought she needed was all that was on my mind, but toward the end of our marriage, I realized that what I *thought* she needed was quite different from what she *really needed*. Her physical needs and what she needed emotionally were two different things, and it was very challenging for her to express that truth to me as her husband.

Our level of communication had tanked, and we were left with two hurt individuals who were married and living under the same roof. Stacey faced changes as a woman and decided that she could no longer be satisfied with who I was as a husband. She believed that as our children were leaving the house to attend their respective colleges, she would find herself alone in a house with a husband who didn't know her at all. My wife felt deeply within her heart that if a change was going to take place in our marriage, then she would have to be the one to make that change. She told me on many occasions that she had come to the resolve that she no longer needed what I had to offer as her husband, because it had become unsatisfying and unfulfilling, to say the least.

Working on marital issues takes an extreme amount of longsuffering, constant communication, and much prayer. The vicissitudes of life had become very difficult for us to navigate. When one's patience wears thin, it leaves the entire marriage vulnerable. Often, when people are involved in a troubled relationship and don't know what to do next, they usually turn to what is either **familiar, comfortable, safe,** or **fantasized**. Stacey had support from all of these areas regarding her marital decision-making process, and regardless of what God or any of the marriage counselors had to say, those images in her mind would always seem to prevail at the end of the day. Those images became the mirror in which she saw our marriage, and each image became a different mirror!

- *The Familiar Image* – She would see our marriage through the image of her parents' failed marriage.

Mentally, she would notice some similarities in the way she felt I had treated her, which reminded her of some of the damaging things her father had taken her mother through, both morally and emotionally. She would constantly defend her actions toward me by saying, "I responded to our emotional upheaval in the same way that I have seen my mother respond toward my father, and it was all that I knew to do!"

- *The Comfortable Image* – She would see our marriage through the image of the dysfunctional marriage of one of her closest friends. Mentally, she would notice an eerie level of comfortability with the emotional separation her friend's marriage had undergone. Although they were living together and legally married, they had lived separate lives for over ten years without the public's knowledge. More recently, they had physically separated by living at a different residence, and they both lived their lives comfortably while remaining legally married. This image was comfortable for Stacey to accept, because it gave her the strength she needed in her resolve about our marital situation.

- *The Safe Image* – My wife no longer felt a sense of safety in her life because of how unstable my style of decision making, and methods of operation had become because of our troubled marriage. She believed she had allowed me to become her god, simply because she had relied on me to do everything as the husband. Her mind was made up, and she believed that now she would solely rely on God as the source of her safety. She felt that if God was going to do anything for her from this point on, He would have to do it without the assistance of me as her husband.

- *The Fantasy Image* – At a very young age, my wife was exposed to images of some very sexually explicit content on television, which developed into her having a fascination with sensual romance novels. She knew early on what kind of relationship she wanted when she got older, for those images would forever become etched in her mind. Because she was raised in a religious environment, her parents were very strict on dating, and although she had dated a few different guys, none of those relationships turned out to be serious until she met me. Her father would often say to people, "From the first time that I saw him, I knew that this would be my daughter's husband!"

We were undoubtedly a model couple for all who knew us, but during the last quarter of our marriage (behind closed doors), we were silently becoming unraveled at the marital seams. Often during times of emotional upheaval, the images trapped in her mind were revived, and those images became a hidden source of refuge. When people have become over-whelmed with a strong sense of lack of fulfillment, frustra-tion, fear, uncertainty, and loss of hope, their minds have the tendency to become vulnerable and violated.

At the end, I realized that I could never measure up to the image that had consumed her mind, and it was evident that I could never do enough on my own to change that scenario. Although I was the epitome of fatherhood for our children, and a paragon of provision for our family, in the end, I fell far short of being the husband that she had always envisioned for herself.

When a person becomes emotionally unraveled, "painted mirrors" can become an escape mechanism. Where there is a lack in the area of natural fulfillment, the body can trick the mind into believing that it can find feelings of fulfilment with an image. The pain of lack of fulfillment is very real, and if that pain becomes persistent, it can lure one into aggres-sively seeking relief by any means necessary. Most people don't regard a fantasy as an act of immorality, because a real person wasn't involved. Here is what the Word of God says about the matter:

> *Ye have heard that it was said by them of old*
> *time, Thou shalt not commit adultery: But I*

say unto you, **That whosoever looketh on a woman to lust after her hath committed adultery with her already in his heart**. *And if thy right eye offend thee, pluck it out, and cast it from thee: for it is profitable for thee that one of thy members should perish, and not that thy whole body should be cast into hell. And if thy right hand offend thee, cut it off, and cast it from thee: for it is profitable for thee that one of thy members should perish, and not that thy whole body should be cast into hell. It hath been said, Whosoever shall put away his wife, let him give her a writing of divorcement:* **But I say unto you, That whosoever shall put away his wife,** <u>**saving for the cause of fornication**</u>, *causeth her to commit adultery: and whosoever shall marry her that is divorced committeth adultery.*

Matthew 5:27-32

The Pharisees also came unto him, tempting him, and saying unto him, Is it lawful for a man to put away his wife for every cause? And he answered and said unto them, Have ye not read, that he which made them at the beginning made them male and female, And said, For *this cause shall a man leave father and mother, and shall cleave to his wife: and they twain shall be one flesh? Wherefore they are no more twain, but one flesh. What therefore God hath joined together, let not man put asunder. They say unto him, Why did Moses then command to give a writing of divorcement, and to put her away? He saith unto them, Moses because of the hardness of your hearts suffered you to put away your wives: but from the beginning it was not so. And I say unto you, **Whosoever shall put away his wife**, <u>**except it be for fornication**</u>, and shall marry another, committeth adultery: and whoso marrieth her which is put away doth commit adultery.*

Matthew 19:3-9

In 2017, Stacey asked me for **a separation**, but I sensed that we had been separated long before she even put in the request! For in 2014, she had already separated from me **mentally** through her lack of intimacy as a wife; in 2016, she had already separated from me **spiritually** by leaving the church where we both pastored; and in 2017, she had already separated from me **physically** by leaving our home and moving in with her sister's family. This request for separation from

Stacey was nothing more than embracing a strong desire to live life as a single individual.

Unfortunately, I couldn't mentally grant her that request, so I divorced Stacey on February 8, 2018. That was the worse day of my life, because I had to let go of the one person, I loved more than any other person on the entire planet! I was very angry with God for a long time and lost my desire to pastor at the church. I had never felt this kind of pain before, and I wasn't sure that I could ever survive it. I would often have conversations with negative spirits such as suicide, murder, depression, loneliness, hatred, worthlessness, and abandonment, just to name a few. But every time I felt those spirits invading my head space, the Spirit of God who dwells within me would see me through those rough times!

I was left wounded and confused, because I thought that I did everything right as a Christian husband. I was a great provider for our family, an excellent father to our children, a faithful husband to my wife, and a caring pastor to the members of our church!

I didn't think that I or Stacey deserved to go through this type of embarrassment, having to face all those people who looked up to us! I was angry with God for this one, because even though we both had our own personal foibles (a minor weakness or eccentricity in someone's character), none of them were deemed unforgiveable! I was angry with God for a long time.

I still believe in holiness, so I choose to remain celibate after the divorce and continue to live according to the parameters of holiness (outlined in the Word of God). I'm not looking for another woman, and I am not interested in joining any of the popular Christian dating sites. I don't *date,* because I simply *wait* for God to send me who He wants me to have! I would be a bald-faced liar if I told you that it is easy to live a life of holiness in this present day! The fact remains that it is unequivocally difficult to live a holy and separated life, but I have found out that the Holy Spirit will keep you even through those times of human weakness.

I begged God to please reveal unto me why we had to go through such a travesty. He told me that I was called to suffer many things for His name's sake and that He knew He could rely on me to come through it and yet remain faithful! So, as I yield to the voice of God and pray daily that I will be found in His perfect will, I now thank Him instead of complaining about the thorn that I have been given in my flesh. I will continue to praise Him, for His grace is enough, for I would only hope that **"my pain"** can be used for **"your gain"**!

Chapter 7

THE GAIN BEHIND THE LOSS

*Now a certain man was sick, named Lazarus, of Bethany, the town of Mary and her sister Martha. (It was that Mary which anointed the Lord with ointment, and wiped his feet with her hair, whose brother Lazarus was sick.) Therefore his sisters sent unto him, saying, Lord, behold, he whom thou lovest is sick. When Jesus heard that, he said, **This sickness is not unto death**, but for the glory of God, that the Son of God might be glorified thereby. Now Jesus loved Martha, and her sister, and Lazarus.*

John 11:1-5

On the surface, the biblical reference found in *John 11:1-5* shows that what has occurred to a good person came by way of the natural evolution of sickness, but (in the spirit realm) it was all

91

orchestrated by God and done simply for His glory. The story paints a picture of some devout Christians (Mary, Martha, and Lazarus) who found themselves in a situation that they could no longer manage. After exhausting all their resources, their belief in the healing power of Jesus prompted them to turn their situation over to Him. Can you imagine how they truly felt at that precise moment, when Jesus stayed His hand of relief and allowed things to get progressively worse, even unto death?

As Christians, we often associate the bad things that happen to us with some sort of demonic attack, and never once think that it may be of God's doing. It has been well documented, and I truly believe that God is the supreme authority, and nothing happens to anyone except if He allows it to be so. The ultimate sacrifice for any Christian has always been for God to get the glory out of our lives. We seldom volunteer ourselves to go through difficult times for His name's sake, so there must be times when God allows bad things to happen to good people.

Can you imagine how the biblical characters Joshua and Caleb (who were fully committed to God) must have felt at that precise moment when they realized that they too would have to wander forty years in the wilderness, alongside those who had disobeyed God? And what about the teenaged Joseph, of whom the Bible says the Spirit of God was with him? How do you think he may have felt at that precise moment when he had to endure being betrayed by his own family, wrongfully accused by those he trusted in authority and abandoned by close friends? These and other biblical references helped me to understand that God's ultimate plan regarding my life is not always understood, but it is at times revealed through experiences that are crafted specifically for me to go through.

There are two types of pain: *one that hurts* and *one that alters!* I didn't realize God's purpose for my pain, until I received the revelation from God concerning the pain. I found out that sometimes God must put us through multiple series of painful situations, just to get us to the very point where the pain actually alters us. The culmination of most painful situations normally takes place at a predestined time implemented by God.

Jesus (who is the Christ) had undergone multiple series of painful situations (the pain that hurts) that spanned the entire thirty-three years of His life on earth, and the culmination of His pain happened on the cross at Calvary (the pain that alters). The next time Jesus was seen by earthly men, He had been altered, and subsequently, His predestined painful process was finished. For the Bible says:

*And when Jesus had cried with a loud voice, he
said, Father, into thy hands I commend my spirit:
and having said thus, he gave up the ghost.*

Luke 23:46

*And Jesus came and spake unto them, saying,
All power is given unto me in heaven and in
earth. Go ye therefore, and teach all nations,
baptizing them in the name of the Father, and
of the Son, and of the Holy Ghost: Teaching
them to observe all things whatsoever I have
commanded you: and, lo, I am with you always,
even unto the end of the world. Amen.*

Matthew 28:18-20

My steps were ordered by God before the foundation of
the world, and like Jesus, I had to undergo multiple series of
painful situations (the pain that hurts). For Jesus, the culmination of His pain (the pain that alters) didn't happen until
after He got up from the grave. The culmination of my pain
didn't happen until 2018, after I got up from my own grave-
like experience.

There are two degrees of the type of *pain that alters,* and
the dichotomy of these two degrees is that one pain may alter
you to do something good, while another pain may alter you

to do something bad. During my adolescence, the *pain of poverty* had altered me in a major way, and during that dark period in my life, I chose to become a drug dealer. Seeing my mother go through the *pain of abuse* had altered me in a major way, and I chose to detest my father while allowing the images of his abuse to guide most of my life choices (outlined in Chapter 3).

Pain, like an emotion, is a hypothetical construct, for it cannot be defined nor can it be measured! There really is no such thing as a positive pain or a negative pain. For every pain has the potential of being positive or negative, because it depends on the context in which the pain is being expressed. It is how the pain fits with your environment, and it depends on the appropriateness or inappropriateness of the intensity in which the pain is being received. That is what determines whether a pain is going to be a catalyst for enrichment or is going to breed negativity. Pain primarily originates from three sources: God, Satan, and sin!

For the Bible says:

> *I am the LORD, and there is none else, there is*
> *no God beside me: I girded thee, though thou*
> *has not known me: That they may know from the*
> *rising of the sun, and from the west, that there*
> *is none beside me. I am the LORD, and there is*

none else. I form the light, and create darkness: I make peace, and create evil: I the LORD do all these things.

Isaiah 45:5-7

Then Satan answered the LORD, and said, Doth Job fear God for nought? Hast not thou made an hedge about him, and about his house, and about all that he hath on every side? Thou hast blessed the work of his hands, and his substance is increased in the land. But put forth thine hand now, and touch all that he hath, and he will curse thee to thy face. And the LORD said unto Satan, Behold, all that he hath is in thy power; only upon himself put not forth thine hand. So Satan went forth from the presence of the LORD.

Job 1:9-12

And unto Adam he said, Because thou hast hearkened unto the voice of thy wife, and hast eaten of the tree, of which I commanded thee, saying, Thou shall not eat of it: cursed is the ground for thy sake; in sorrow shalt thou eat of it all the days of thy life;

Genesis 3:17

The issue now becomes: How do we respond to the pain? God wants us to respond in a positive way, by bringing Him glory despite the pain. Satan wants us to respond in a negative way, by cursing God to His face because of the pain, while sin wants us to respond in a humanistic way, by hiding from God in lieu of the pain. Pain can act as a buffer to remind us that God's grace is enough. Pain can also bring about true repentance, or pain could lead a person toward a spiritual disconnect from God.

It is a fact that pain is an inevitable experience that everyone must go through, and yet the degree of the pain is different for every individual. Causality is the relationship between a cause and an effect, which supports the principle that everything has a cause. In Christianity, we are not judged by God on the cause; rather, we are judged on our response to the effect! No matter how many scriptural references I find, valid points I make, proof of evidence I provide, or excuses I come up with, my response has always been what matters to God.

The issue now becomes: What is it that lies within me that seems to provoke me to respond in a disorderly fashion toward God? I love God with all my heart, and I truly pride myself on being a man after His own heart. God asked me: How can I say that I love Him, and not do the things He tells me to do? Without trying to defend myself, I asked God to explain what He was speaking about. He simply replied, "You have yet to completely surrender yourself to me!" As I pondered His response, I was silenced by the mere fact that I had done something that made God think I didn't truly love Him.

To be made speechless was a rare occasion for me, but wisdom would see fit to bridle my tongue and force me to meditate on what God said. The process of understanding exactly what God was trying to say or do regarding my life had become very challenging because of what I call "the hecklers of life." Hecklers are those hidden emotions, thoughts, and spirits that act as critics, interrupters, and troublemakers. The purpose of these hecklers is to distort the interpretation of God's Word by the Holy Spirit. The Holy Spirit leads and guides us into all truth, while giving us firsthand knowledge of what God has said.

There are times when my emotions just don't agree with what God is saying. There are times when my mind can't comprehend whatever God is doing. There are times when the cravings of my flesh want that thing God says I can't have. And there are times when Satan presents a more interesting argument than God does (mostly when I'm feeling carnal). During those flare-ups, my emotions, intellect, body, and those demonic forces become "the hecklers of life" by distorting, and at times overriding, what the Holy Spirit is speaking to me.

Without justifying it, I had grown accustomed to those flare-ups, to the point that they had become a part of my character. I must confess that God was right. I really hadn't fully committed myself to Him like I should have. At some of the most critical times, my internal struggles, along with the vivid negative images of my past, were just too much for me to bear. Unbeknownst to me, the internal battles that I had lost were outweighing those external battles that I had won and prevented me from maximizing my God-given potential. The apostle Paul puts it this way:

> *For I delight in the law of God after the inward man: But I see another law in my members, warring against the law of my mind, and bringing me into captivity to the law of sin which is in my members. O wretched man that I am! Who shall deliver me from the body of this death?*
>
> *Romans 7:22-24*

I just didn't know how to break the vicious cycle, and I would often find myself fasting and praying to God for help. Relief would come, but often in the form of grace and mercy instead of deliverance. Getting me through something is quite different from delivering me from something. My internal battles seemed to be more prevalent when my mind was not focused on the things of God. For when pain affects my mind, body, and spirit simultaneously, it renders me helpless when it comes to keeping my mind focused on God.

> *Therefore take no thought, saying, What shall we eat? Or, What shall we drink? Or, Wherewithal shall we be clothed? (For after all these things do the Gentiles seek:) for your heavenly Father knoweth that ye have need of all these things.* ***But seek ye first*** *the kingdom of God, and his righteousness; and all these things shall be added unto you.*
>
> Matthew 6:31-33

Doing those things, I *believe* God wants me to do is not the same as doing those things I *know* God told me to do. I see now that the reason why I had not completely surrendered to God was not due to a lack of obedience, but rather a lack of seeking Him first. When the pain of my past would correlate with my current pain, that connection would often sway me to make decisions that I believed to be right. The illusion that any action is progress would at various times invade my heart and lead me to do what I felt was right.

*For I know the thoughts that I think towards you, saith the Lord, thoughts of peace, and not of evil, to give you **an expected end**. Then shall ye <u>call upon me</u>, and ye shall go and <u>pray unto me</u>, and I will hearken unto you. And ye shall <u>seek me</u>, and find me, when ye shall <u>search for me</u> **with all your heart**.*

Jeremiah 29:11-13

My recurring emotional flare-ups would often derail me as I traveled on the path that God prepared in route to my expected end. Following God to wherever He led me was not an issue for me, but my problem was: How do I remain focused and remain "guidable"? It has always been a foible of mine (a character flaw that is normally forgivable), and yet it is a very common flaw in most people.

*And after six days Jesus taketh with him Peter, and James, and John, and leadeth them up into an high mountain apart by themselves: and he was transfigured before them. And his raiment became shining, exceeding white as snow; so as no fuller on earth can white them. And there appeared unto them Elias with Moses: and they were talking with Jesus. And **Peter answered*** *and said to Jesus, Master, it is good for us to be here: and let us make three tabernacles; one for thee, and one for Moses, and one for Elias. For he wist not what to say; for they were sore afraid. And there was a cloud that overshadowed them: and a voice came out of the cloud, saying, This is my beloved Son: **hear him**. And suddenly, when they had looked round about, they saw no man any more, save Jesus only with themselves.*

Mark 9:2-8

In this situation, Peter had lost his focus and allowed his emotions to overwhelm him. Although he spoke candidly about what he was feeling emotionally, God made it clear that it was wrong for him to make that decision. Kingdom decisions are made by persons with kingdom authority, Peter (like us all) was subjugated under the authority of Jesus. The Holy Trinity (God the Father, God the Son, and God the Holy Spirit) all act as one supreme authority. Since Peter was with Jesus at the time, God spoke from the cloud, saying, "This is My beloved Son. Listen only to Him." I believe that as Christians, we have been given authority (dominion) in the Earth, but Jesus has been given all power (supreme authority) both in Heaven and on the Earth.

*And Jesus came and spake unto them, saying, All
power is given unto me in heaven and in earth.*
                                            Matthew 28:18

No one could say exactly what Peter was going through at
that precise moment, but whatever it was, it was strong enough
to have him speak without consulting Jesus. There were many
occasions that I acted without consulting Jesus, and every time
I did so, it felt like the right thing to do. Sometimes we can
put the cart before the horse by acting on things relating to our
Kingdom assignments, before we have been given the proper
authority to do so. It only takes a split second for anyone to
lose focus on God, and it takes God to help us get re-focused.
The only way to get Peter re-focused and re-guidable was for
God to take away some of the visible objects of his affection.

*And suddenly, when they had looked round
about, they saw no man any more, save Jesus
only with themselves.*
                                            Mark 9:8

My life had become volatile! I was disgruntled with the
vicissitudes of life, plagued by the images of my past, and
my spirit had been badly wounded. I had now switched to a
survival mode of living, for I found myself on a path of no

return. And the only way that God could get me refocused and back to being guidable was by removing some of the things that had become the source of my distraction. It is not the situation that determines whether I become distracted and lose my focus on God; it's what I believe about the situation that ultimately leads to my distraction! My beliefs had been shaped by my past experiences, my emotions, and my limited knowledge. Once I had truly believed something to be so, I would respond according to that belief, and rarely did I seek God prior to my actions.

Because my heart was good as a person, I would often do things with good intentions and not seek the authority to do it. Because I did a lot of things with good intentions, I became misguided in my thinking. I felt emotionally that doing a "good thing" was the same as doing a "God thing," but now I know that it's not true. I had to find out the hard way, because I had done so many good things for many people, and most occurred after I got saved in 1990.

God requires me to seek Him first, and His righteousness and everything that I need will be added unto me. I say that "God requires me" to seek Him first, because there are many people who seemingly get away with things that I couldn't get away with! I was a good servant in my church; I was a good husband; I was a good father; I was a good employee; I was a good person in the community, but all that did not exempt me from seeking God first! A good thing done through the heart can turn out to be a bad thing if not done through prayer. God had to remind me that in all my ways, I had to acknowledge Him and allow Him to direct my path.

I was an all-around good person, but according to God, I did too many things from the heart and out of my emotions. The quest now for me was to recognize the origin of the source of my distractions and to bring it under subjection to the will of God. This quest would take me back to my childhood and through my adolescence, growing up poor in the inner city. The damage that I incurred during those periods of my life would prove to play a major role regarding my actions and reactions. Doing things in the present because of my past experiences had become the foundation of my current method of operation.

God had performed so many miraculous things in my life to ensure that I would get to the point in my life where I would recognize who He truly is. He is not just the Lord of my religion; He's the Lord of my life. God was jealous, because after giving me His all, I had not reciprocated the gesture by giving Him my all. Trust, loyalty, and obedience are major acts of love that I show toward God, and when I go astray from those acts of love, it hurts Him.

God had never failed me! So, His track record of being there for me was not the issue. The issue was how could I allow any situation to become so overwhelming that it drew me away from God? There had been many times that I didn't trust God, because I felt that His way was not conducive to my way at the time. Whether it was because of some past pain, emotional upheaval, psychological trauma, or spiritual attack, I chose not to trust God on many occasions. I was taught through the Word of God to trust in the Lord with all my heart, with all my soul, and with all my mind. I could not lean to my own understanding, but in all my ways acknowledge Him, and He would direct my path. I wasn't strong enough to fight the forces of my human nature, so at times, I found myself trusting in people instead of fully trusting in God.

There had been many times that I wasn't loyal to God, because I felt at times that the love of people was more advantageous. No greater love is there than a man who would lay down his life for a friend, and God did that for the entire world. I was very hypocritical, because I would go out of my way for others, and I would expect their loyalty in return. God had done so much for me, yet my loyalty to Him was not reciprocal. Too many times, I put my needs and wants and the needs and wants of others before God. I never thought of how my actions made God feel, but I was quick to let someone else know how their lack of loyalty made me feel. The frequency of my lack of loyalty toward God was alarming, because it seemed like I did it without guilt or shame. God's method of getting my attention was very methodical, for He would allow my children to treat me in the same manner that I was treating Him. Then I understood how I had made God feel on numerous occasions.

There had been many times I wasn't obedient to God, because I would struggle with doing what I wanted to do. Obedience to God is far greater than any form of human sacrifice, yet I would at times still choose to disobey. There was no explanation, other than I had simply made a choice, for at the end of the day, the choice was mine to be made. The process of how I made my choices was in desperate need of alteration. God would speak to me about what He desired me to do in various ways, yet at times I would allow my desires to prevail. As for me, pain, pride, selfish desires, and fear were just some of the things that tipped the "scale of my decision making" toward disobedience. I know now what a wretched man feels like and constantly pray that I would overcome this feeling long before I meet God face to face.

What caused me to stagger regarding my relationship with God were some critical things from my past that had never been noticed or resolved. My past experiences, images of painful moments, and unwarranted beliefs were paving a difficult road for me to travel. I had become so comfortable with my flaws that they didn't even seem like flaws at all. I never saw that I had unresolved issues beneath the layers of life, simply because when one thing didn't work out, I just moved on to the next thing. God had to get my attention this one last time, before I was completely derailed from my road to destiny. God knows what plans He has for me, and I was on the brink of destroying those plans for good.

> *But what things were gain to me, those I counted* ***loss*** *for Christ. Yea doubtless, and I count all things but* ***loss*** *for the excellency of the knowledge of Christ Jesus my Lord: for whom I have suffered the* ***loss*** *of all things, and do count them but dung, that I may win Christ. And be found in him, not having mine own righteousness, which is of the law, but that which is through the faith of Christ, the righteousness which is of God by faith.*
>
> *Philippians 3:7-9*

Loss was not new to me, for I had lost many things over the years and I had survived by the simple act of replacement. My mind, during any loss, is normally focused on that thing I lost. God now wanted to shift my focus, not on the external thing that was lost but on the "internal reason" why it was lost. I never thought to look within me for the reason behind the loss. It wasn't pride or arrogance that kept me from looking within; it was simply my ignorance of those things that kept me bond.

It wasn't until the loss of my marriage after twenty-three years, and loss of the church where I pastored for fifteen years, that I realized I had possessed some deeply rooted issues. All the good that I had accomplished within the marriage and at the church had blinded me to the bad things that internally lay dormant. God knew that to regain a right relationship with Him, I would have to address those internal issues one way or another.

I would often identify the problems of other people and the personal problems they had with me. But God showed me that the real problem originated because of my internal issues. I could not control the internal issues that others had; I could only address those found within me. So, in theory, I had to suffer tremendous loss for such a time as this, to gain a right spirit as I journey toward my expected end.

The "gain behind the loss" was very painful, to say the least, but I've learned that through it all, **"my pain"** was for **"your gain."**

CPSIA information can be obtained
at www.ICGtesting.com
Printed in the USA
BVHW071937230519
549175BV00001B/3/P

9 781545 666609